On
Trust

HBR's 10 Must Reads series is the definitive collection of ideas and best practices for aspiring and experienced leaders alike. These books offer essential reading selected from the pages of *Harvard Business Review* on topics critical to the success of every manager.

Titles include:

HBR's 10 Must Reads 2015
HBR's 10 Must Reads 2016
HBR's 10 Must Reads 2017
HBR's 10 Must Reads 2018
HBR's 10 Must Reads 2019
HBR's 10 Must Reads 2020
HBR's 10 Must Reads 2021
HBR's 10 Must Reads 2022
HBR's 10 Must Reads 2023
HBR's 10 Must Reads for CEOs
HBR's 10 Must Reads for New Managers
HBR's 10 Must Reads on AI, Analytics, and the New Machine Age
HBR's 10 Must Reads on Boards
HBR's 10 Must Reads on Building a Great Culture
HBR's 10 Must Reads on Business Model Innovation
HBR's 10 Must Reads on Career Resilience
HBR's 10 Must Reads on Change Management (Volumes 1 and 2)
HBR's 10 Must Reads on Collaboration
HBR's 10 Must Reads on Communication (Volumes 1 and 2)
HBR's 10 Must Reads on Creativity
HBR's 10 Must Reads on Design Thinking
HBR's 10 Must Reads on Diversity
HBR's 10 Must Reads on Emotional Intelligence
HBR's 10 Must Reads on Entrepreneurship and Startups
HBR's 10 Must Reads on High Performance
HBR's 10 Must Reads on Innovation
HBR's 10 Must Reads on Leadership (Volumes 1 and 2)
HBR's 10 Must Reads on Leadership for Healthcare

On
Trust

HARVARD BUSINESS REVIEW PRESS
Boston, Massachusetts

Library of Congress Cataloging-in-Publication Data

Names: Harvard Business Review Press, issuing body.
Title: HBR's 10 must reads on trust / Harvard Business Review.
Other titles: Harvard business review's ten must reads on trust | HBR's 10 must reads (Series)
Description: Boston, Massachusetts : Harvard Business Review Press, [2023] | Series: HBR's 10 must reads | Includes index. |
Identifiers: LCCN 2022038641 (print) | LCCN 2022038642 (ebook) | ISBN 9781647825249 (paperback) | ISBN 9781647825256 (epub)
Subjects: LCSH: Trust. | Business ethics. | Success in business.
Classification: LCC BF575.T7 .H38 2023 (print) | LCC BF575.T7 (ebook) | DDC 179/.9—dc23/eng/20221017
LC record available at https://lccn.loc.gov/2022038641
LC ebook record available at https://lccn.loc.gov/2022038642

Contents

HBR'S 10 MUST READS

On
Trust

Begin with Trust

by Frances X. Frei and Anne Morriss

ON A SPRING AFTERNOON IN 2017, Travis Kalanick, then the CEO of Uber, walked into a conference room at the company's Bay Area headquarters. One of us, Frances, was waiting for him. Meghan Joyce, the company's general manager for the United States and Canada, had reached out to us, hoping that we could guide the company as it sought to heal from a series of deep, self-inflicted wounds. We had a track record of helping organizations, many of them founder-led, tackle messy leadership and culture challenges.

We were skeptical about Uber. Everything we'd read about the company suggested it had little hope of redemption. At the time, the company was an astonishingly disruptive and successful start-up, but its success seemed to have come at the price of basic decency. In early 2017, for example, when taxi drivers went on strike in New York City to protest President Trump's travel ban, Uber appeared to have used tactics to profit from the situation—a move that prompted widespread outrage and a #deleteUber campaign. A month later, not long before the meeting, an Uber engineer named Susan Fowler had blogged courageously about her experiences of harassment and discrimination at the company, which caused more outrage. Footage of Kalanick had then emerged, in a video that went viral, of his interaction with an Uber driver, where he appeared dismissive of the pain of earning a living in a post-Uber world. Additional charges leveled at the company in this period reinforced Uber's reputation as a cold-blooded operator that would do almost anything to win.

Despite our skepticism, Frances had gone to California to hear Kalanick out. (Anne was building her own company at the time, so

1

she took a back seat on the project.) As Frances waited for him to make his entrance, she braced herself for the smug CEO she'd read about. But that wasn't who walked in. Kalanick arrived humbled and introspective. He had thought a lot about how the cultural values he'd instilled in the company—the very values that had fueled Uber's success—had also been misused and distorted on his watch. He expressed deep respect for what his team had achieved but also acknowledged that he'd put some people in leadership roles without giving them the training or mentorship to be effective. Whatever mistakes Kalanick had made up to that point, he revealed a sincere desire to do the right thing as a leader.

We regrouped back in Cambridge, Massachusetts, and debated whether to take on the project. There were lots of reasons to stay far away from it. The work would be hard and its outcome uncertain, to say nothing of the brutal commute. Uber's workforce was frustrated, and the brand was becoming toxic. But we realized that if we could help get Uber back on the right path, then we could offer a road map to countless others trying to restore humanity to organizations that had lost their way. So we signed on.

After making that decision, we knew exactly where to start. With trust.

Empowerment Leadership

We think of trust as precious, and yet it's the basis for almost everything we do as civilized people. Trust is the reason we're willing to exchange our hard-earned paychecks for goods and services, pledge our lives to another person in marriage, cast a ballot for someone who will represent our interests. We rely on laws and contracts as safety nets, but even they are ultimately built on trust in the institutions that enforce them. We don't know that justice will be served if something goes wrong, but we have enough faith in the system that we're willing to make high-stakes deals with relative strangers.

Trust is also one of the most essential forms of capital a leader has. Building trust, however, often requires thinking about leadership from a new perspective. The traditional leadership narrative

Idea in Brief

The Starting Point

The traditional leadership narrative is all about you: your talents, charisma, and moments of courage and instinct. But real leadership is about your people and creating the conditions for them to fully realize their own capacity and power. To do this, you have to develop stores of trust.

The Challenge

How do leaders build trust? By focusing on its core drivers: authenticity, logic, and empathy.

People tend to trust you when they think they're interacting with the real you, when they have faith in your judgment and competence, and when they believe you care about them.

The Way Forward

When leaders have trouble with trust, it's usually because they're weak on one of those three drivers. To develop or restore trust, identify which driver you're "wobbly" on, and then work on strengthening it.

is all about you: your vision and strategy; your ability to make the tough calls and rally the troops; your talents, your charisma, your heroic moments of courage and instinct. But leadership really isn't about you. It's about empowering other people as a result of your presence, and about making sure that the impact of your leadership continues into your absence.

That's the fundamental principle we've learned in the course of dedicating our careers to making leaders and organizations better. Your job as a leader is to create the conditions for your people to fully realize their own capacity and power. And that's true not only when you're in the trenches with them but also when you're not around and even—this is the cleanest test—when you've permanently moved on from the team. We call it empowerment leadership. The more trust you build, the more possible it is to practice this kind of leadership.

The Core Drivers of Trust

So how do you build up stores of this foundational leadership capital? In our experience, trust has three core drivers: authenticity, logic, and empathy. People tend to trust you when they believe they are interacting with the real you (authenticity), when they have faith in your judgment and competence (logic), and when they feel that you care about them (empathy). When trust is lost, it can almost always be traced back to a breakdown in one of these three drivers.

People don't always realize how the information (or more often, the misinformation) that they're broadcasting may undermine their own trustworthiness. What's worse, stress tends to amplify the problem, causing people to double down on behaviors that make others skeptical. For example, they might unconsciously mask their true selves in a job interview, even though that's precisely the type of less-than-fully-authentic behavior that reduces their chance of being hired.

The good news is that most of us generate a stable pattern of trust signals, which means a small change in behavior can go a long way. In moments when trust is broken, or fails to get any real traction, it's usually the same driver that has gone wobbly on us—authenticity, empathy, or logic. We call this driver your "trust wobble." In simple terms, it's the driver that's most likely to fail you.

Everybody, it turns out, has a trust wobble. To build trust as a leader, you first need to figure out what yours is.

Build It, and They Will Come

To identify your wobble, think of a recent moment when you were not trusted as much as you wanted to be. Maybe you lost an important sale or didn't get a stretch assignment. Maybe someone simply doubted your ability to execute. With that moment in mind, do something hard: Give the other person in your story the benefit of the doubt. Let's call that person your "skeptic." Assume that your skeptic's reservations were valid and that you were the one responsible for the breakdown in trust. This exercise only works if you own it.

If you had to choose from our three trust drivers, which would you say went wobbly on you in this situation? Did your skeptic feel you were misrepresenting some part of yourself or your story? If so, that's an authenticity problem. Did your skeptic feel you might be

The trust triangle

Trust has three drivers: authenticity, logic, and empathy. When trust is lost, it can almost always be traced back to a breakdown in one of them. To build trust as a leader, you first need to figure out which driver you "wobble" on.

Authenticity
I experience the real you.

Logic
I know you can do it; your reasoning and judgment are sound.

TRUST

Empathy
I believe you care about me and my success.

putting your own interests first? If so, that's an empathy problem. Did your skeptic question the rigor of your analysis or your ability to execute on an ambitious plan? If so, that's a logic problem.

Now stand back and try to look at your pattern of wobbles across multiple incidents. Pick three or four interactions that stand out to you, for whatever reason, and do a quick trust diagnostic for each one. What does your typical wobble seem to be? Does the pattern change under stress or with different kinds of stakeholders? For example, do you wobble on one trait with your direct reports but on a different one with people who have authority over you? That's not uncommon.

This exercise works best if you bring at least one person along for your diagnostic ride, ideally someone who knows you well. Sharing your analysis can be clarifying—even liberating—and will help you test and refine your hypothesis. In our experience, about 20% of self-assessments need a round of revision, so choose a partner who can keep you honest. Consider going back and testing your analysis directly by speaking openly about it with your skeptic. This conversation alone can be a powerful way to rebuild trust. When you take responsibility for a wobble, you reveal your humanity (authenticity) and analytic chops (logic) while communicating your commitment to the relationship (empathy).

Overcoming Your Wobble

Over the past decade we've helped all kinds of leaders—from seasoned politicians to Millennial entrepreneurs to the heads of multibillion-dollar companies—wrestle with trust issues. In doing so, we've learned a lot about strategies you can deploy to overcome your own trust wobbles. Let's explore what's most effective for each of the drivers in our trust triangle.

Empathy

Most high-achieving leaders struggle with this one. Signaling a lack of empathy is a major barrier to empowerment leadership. If people think you care more about yourself than about others, they won't trust you enough to lead them.

Empathy wobbles are common among people who are analytical and driven to learn. They often get impatient with those who aren't similarly motivated or who take longer than they do to understand something. Additionally, the tools and experience of the modern workplace continually distract or prevent us from demonstrating empathy, by imposing 24-hour demands on our time and putting at our disposal all sorts of technologies that compete for our attention at any given moment. Our beeping and buzzing devices constantly assert our self-importance, sometimes smack in the middle of interactions with the very people we're working to empower and lead.

We advise empathy wobblers to pay close attention to their behavior in group settings, particularly when other people have the floor. Consider what often happens in a meeting: When it kicks off, most people feel very engaged. But as soon as empathy wobblers understand the concepts under discussion and have contributed their ideas, they lose interest. Their engagement plummets and remains low until the gathering (mercifully) comes to an end. Instead of paying attention, they often multitask, check their phones, engage in flamboyant displays of boredom—anything to make clear that this meeting is beneath them. Unfortunately, the cost of these indulgences is trust. If you signal that you matter more than everyone else, why should anyone trust the direction you're going in? What's in it for the rest of us to come along?

There's a basic solution to this problem. Instead of focusing on what you need in that meeting, work to ensure that everyone else gets what they need. Take radical responsibility for the others in the room. Share the burden of moving the dialogue forward, even if it's not your meeting. Search for the resonant examples that will bring the concepts to life, and don't disengage until everyone else in the room understands. This is almost impossible to do if texting or checking email is an option, so put away your devices. Everyone knows you're not taking notes on their good ideas.

Indeed, the last thing we'll say on empathy is this: If you do nothing else to change your behavior, put away your phone more frequently. Put it truly away, out of sight and out of reach, not just flipped over for a few minutes at a time. You'll be amazed at the change in the quality of your interactions and your ability to build trust.

Logic

If people don't always have confidence in the rigor of your ideas, or if they don't have full faith in your ability to deliver on them, then logic is probably your wobble. If they don't trust your judgment, why would they want you at the wheel?

When logic is the problem, we advise going back to the data. Root the case you're making in sound evidence, speak about the things you know to be true beyond a reasonable doubt, and then—this is the hard part—stop there. One reason Larry Bird was such an extraordinary basketball player was that he only took shots he knew he could reliably make. That choice made him different from other great players who let ego and adrenaline cloud their shooting judgment. Bird studied and practiced so relentlessly that by the time the ball left his hands in the heat of competition, he knew exactly where it was going. If logic is your wobble, take Bird's example and learn to "play within yourself."

Once you get comfortable with how that feels, start expanding what you know. Along the way, make an effort to learn from other people. Their insight is among your most valuable resources, but to access it, you must be willing to reveal that you don't have all the answers—something leaders often resist. Engaging people about their experience has the additional benefit of communicating who you are and what energizes you professionally—an authenticity boost.

For most logic wobblers, however, rigor isn't the issue. Much of the time, the problem is the perception of wobbly logic rather than the reality of it. Why does this happen? Because they're not communicating their ideas effectively.

There are generally two ways to communicate complex thoughts. The first takes your audience on a journey, with twists and turns and context and dramatic tension, until they eventually get to the payoff. Many of the world's best storytellers use this technique. You can visualize this approach by imagining an inverted triangle. The journeying storyteller starts at the top, at the inverted base of the triangle, and traces an enchantingly meandering route down to its point.

If logic is your wobble, however, that's a risky path to take. With all that circuitous journeying, you're likely to lose your audience along the way rather than build trust in your judgment. Listeners may even abandon you at one of your narrative turns.

To avoid that, try flipping the imaginary triangle upright. Start with your main point, or headline, at the top of the triangle, and then work your way down, building a base of reinforcing evidence. This approach signals a clarity of vision and a full command of the facts. Everyone has a much better chance of following your logic. Even if you get interrupted along the way, you'll at least have had a chance to communicate your key idea.

Authenticity
If people feel they're not getting access to the "real" you—to a full and complete accounting of what you know, think, and feel—then you probably have an authenticity wobble.

A quick test: How different is your professional persona from the one that shows up around family and friends? If there's a sharp difference, what are you getting in return for masking or minimizing certain parts of yourself? What's the payoff?

Being your "real self" sounds nice in theory, but there can be powerful reasons for holding back certain truths. The calculation can be highly practical at times, if wrenching—as in deciding to stay closeted in a workplace that's hostile to queer identities. There may also be times when expressing your authentic feelings may risk harmful consequences: Women, for example, are disproportionately penalized for displaying negative emotions in the workplace, and Black men are burdened by the false stereotype that they are predisposed to anger. We're not talking here about moments of prudent self-censorship, which sometimes can't be divorced from a larger context of bias or low psychological safety. Instead, we're talking about inauthenticity as a strategy, a way of navigating the workplace. If this is how you operate, you're dealing with an authenticity wobble.

In our experience, although withholding your true self may sometimes help you solve problems in the short term, it puts an artificial cap on trust and, by extension, on your ability to lead. When people sense that you're concealing the truth or being less than authentic, they're far less willing to make themselves vulnerable to you in the ways that leadership demands.

We've observed the cost of inauthenticity up close in the performance of diverse teams. Diversity can be a tremendous asset in today's marketplace, and the companies that get it right often enjoy powerful competitive tailwinds. But this advantage isn't automatic. Simply populating your team with diverse perspectives and experiences doesn't always translate into better performance. In fact, the uncomfortable truth is that diverse teams can underperform homogenous teams if they're not managed actively for differences among members. That is due in part to a phenomenon called the common information effect, which works like this: As human beings, we tend to focus on the things we have in common with other people. We tend to seek out and affirm our shared knowledge, because it confirms our value and kinship with the group. Diverse teams, by definition, have less common information readily available to them to use in collective decision-making.

Consider two teams of three people, one in which the three members are different from one another, and the other in which they're similar. If both teams are managed in exactly the same way—if they simply follow the same best practices in group facilitation, for example—the homogenous team is likely to perform better. No amount of feedback or number of trust falls can overcome the strength of the common information effect.

But the effect only holds if people wobble on authenticity. When they choose to bring their unique selves to the table—that is, the parts of themselves that are different from other people—they can create an unbeatable advantage by expanding the amount of information the team can access. The result is an inclusive team that's likely to outperform (by a long shot) both homogenous teams and diverse teams that aren't actively managed for inclusion. (See the exhibit "Trust, diversity, and team performance.")

This expansion of knowledge and its obvious benefits rely on the courage of authenticity wobblers. We know how difficult sharing who we really are can be, and we also know that it's sometimes too much to ask. But if we regularly give in to the pressure to hold back our unique selves, then we suppress the most valuable parts of ourselves. Not only do we end up concealing the very thing the world needs most from us—our differences—but we also make it harder for people to trust us as leaders.

Here's the reason to care, even if you don't see yourself as different: All of us pay the price of inauthentic interactions, and all of us have a better chance of thriving in inclusive environments where authenticity can flourish. Gender bias, in other words, is not just a woman's problem. Systemic racism is not just an African American or Latinx problem. It's our shared moral and organizational imperative to create workplaces where the burdens of being different are shouldered by all of us. After all, we will all benefit wildly from eliminating them.

Trust, diversity, and team performance

Diversity doesn't automatically confer advantages in decision-making. In fact, if diverse teams aren't managed actively for inclusion, they can un- derperform homogenous ones. That's because shared knowledge is key in decision-making, and diverse teams, by definition, start out with less of it. But if you create conditions of trust that allow diverse team members to bring their unique perspectives and experiences to the table, you can expand the amount of knowledge your team can access—and create an unbeatable advantage.

Diverse teams
A diverse store of knowledge is partly shared.

Homogenous teams
A common store of knowledge is fully shared.

Inclusive teams
A diverse store of knowledge is fully shared.

One of the lessons we've learned in our work with organizations is that creating spaces where authenticity can thrive is not as hard as it may seem. It is an urgent, achievable goal that requires far less audacity than disrupting industries or growing complex organizations— things leaders do every day with deep conviction in the outcomes. If all of us take responsibility for creating companies where difference can thrive, and all of us take responsibility for showing up in them authentically, then our chances of achieving true inclusion—and building high levels of trust—start to look pretty good.

So pay less attention to what you think people want to hear and more attention to what you need to say to them. Reveal your full humanity to the world, regardless of what your critics say. And while you're at it, take exquisite care of people who are different from you, confident in the knowledge that their difference is the very thing that could unleash your potential and your organization's.

In Myself I Trust

We've argued that the foundation of empowerment leadership is getting other people to trust you. That's certainly true, but there's one last thing you need to know. The path to empowerment leadership doesn't begin when other people start to trust you. It begins when you start to trust yourself.

To be a truly empowering leader, you need to take stock of where you wobble not only in your relationships with others but also in your relationship with yourself. Are you being honest with yourself about your ambitions, or are you ignoring what really excites and inspires you? If you're hiding something from yourself, you've got an authenticity problem you need to address. Do you acknowledge your own needs and attend properly to them? If not, you've got to adopt a more empathetic posture toward yourself. Do you lack conviction in your own ideas and ability to perform? If so, you've got some logic issues to work out.

Doing this work is important as a leader, for an arguably obvious reason. If you don't trust yourself, why should anybody else trust you?

A Campaign to Rebuild Trust

Let's now return to Uber. When we began working with the company, it was certainly wobbling—so much so that we diagnosed it as "a hot mess."

What was going on?

Consider the basic trust-related facts. There's no question that Uber had empathy problems. The company's focus on growth at all costs meant that relationships with stakeholders, particularly drivers and employees, needed real attention. Riders also needed to be assured that their safety wouldn't come second to the company's financial performance. Additionally, despite its disruptive success, Uber hadn't answered questions about the long-term viability of its business model or about whether its managers had the skills to lead an organization of its expansive scale and scope. These were unaddressed logic problems. Finally, the company's war-room mentality was undermining its authenticity. In the "us versus them" culture at Uber, people were skeptical that they were getting the full story.

By the time Frances began working with Kalanick, he had already begun making changes to steady the company's trust wobbles. He had hired Eric Holder, for example, who had served as U.S. attorney general under President Obama, to lead a rigorous internal investigation into harassment and discrimination—and when Holder made a sweeping set of recommendations, Kalanick took action to implement them. The company was also on the verge of rolling out new driver-tipping functionality, which would go on to generate $600 million in additional driver compensation in the first year of its launch. New safety features were in development, too, designed to give both drivers and riders additional tools to protect themselves.

Kalanick didn't get the chance to see most of these initiatives to completion, at least not from the CEO chair. In June 2017, he was forced out as CEO, although he retained his board seat and an equity stake in the company until December 2019, when he gave both up. He was ultimately replaced by Dara Khosrowshahi, the former Expedia CEO, who had a track record of effective leadership at the helm of young companies.

Frances soon began working with Khosrowshahi to continue the campaign to rebuild trust internally. Together they led an effort to rewrite the company's cultural values, one that invited input from all 15,000 employees on the principles that they wanted Uber to live by. The new motto they settled on was "We do the right thing. Period." Other early trust wins for Khosrowshahi included strengthening relationships with regulators and executing a logic-driven focus on the services and markets that were most defensible.

Most of the work we did during this period was aimed at rebuilding trust at the employee level. Some things were easy to identify and fix, like ratcheting down the widespread, empathy-pulverizing practice of texting during meetings about the other people in the meeting, a tech-company norm that shocked us when we first experienced it. We introduced a new norm of turning off all personal technology and putting it away during meetings, which forced people to start making eye contact with their colleagues again.

Other challenges were harder to tackle, like the need to upskill thousands of managers. Our take was that Uber had underinvested in its people during its period of hypergrowth, leaving many managers unprepared for the increasing complexity of their jobs. We addressed this logic wobble with a massive infusion of executive education, using a virtual classroom to engage employees in live case discussions—our pedagogy of choice—whether they were in San Francisco, London, or Hyderabad. Although our pilot program was voluntary and classes were sometimes scheduled at absurdly inconvenient times, 6,000 Uber employees based in more than 50 countries each participated in 24 hours of instruction over the course of 60 days. It was an extraordinary pace, scale, and absorption of management education.

The curriculum gave people tools and concepts to develop quickly as leaders while flipping a whole lot of upside-down communication triangles. Employees gained the skills not only to listen better but also to talk in ways that made it easier to collaborate across business units and geographies. Frances went out in the field, visiting key global offices in her first 30 days on the job, carving out protected spaces to listen to employees and communicate leadership's commitment to building a company worthy of its people. At a time when many employees were conflicted about their Uber affiliations, Frances made it a point to wear an Uber T-shirt every day until the entire company was proud to be on the payroll.

Within a year, Uber was less wobbly. There were still problems to be solved, but indicators such as employee sentiment, brand health, and driver compensation were all heading in the right direction, and the march toward an IPO began in earnest. Good people were deciding to stay with the company, more good people were joining, and, in what had become our favorite indicator of progress, an increasing number of Uber T-shirts could now be spotted on city streets. It was all a testament to the talent, creativity, and commitment to learning at every level of the organization—and to the new foundation of trust that Kalanick and Khosrowshahi had been able to build.

Originally published in May–June 2020. Reprint R2003H

The Neuroscience of Trust

by Paul J. Zak

COMPANIES ARE TWISTING THEMSELVES into knots to empower and challenge their employees. They're anxious about the sad state of engagement, and rightly so, given the value they're losing. Consider Gallup's meta-analysis of decades' worth of data: It shows that high engagement—defined largely as having a strong connection with one's work and colleagues, feeling like a real contributor, and enjoying ample chances to learn—consistently leads to positive outcomes for both individuals and organizations. The rewards include higher productivity, better-quality products, and increased profitability.

So it's clear that creating an employee-centric culture can be good for business. But how do you do that effectively? Culture is typically designed in an ad hoc way around random perks like gourmet meals or "karaoke Fridays," often in thrall to some psychological fad. And despite the evidence that you can't buy higher job satisfaction, organizations still use golden handcuffs to keep good employees in place. While such efforts might boost workplace happiness in the short term, they fail to have any lasting effect on talent retention or performance.

In my research I've found that building a culture of trust is what makes a meaningful difference. Employees in high-trust organizations are more productive, have more energy at work, collaborate better with their colleagues, and stay with their employers longer than people working at low-trust companies. They also suffer less chronic stress and are happier with their lives, and these factors fuel stronger performance.

Leaders understand the stakes—at least in principle. In its 2016 global CEO survey, PwC reported that 55% of CEOs think that a lack of trust is a threat to their organization's growth. But most have done little to increase trust, mainly because they aren't sure where to start. In this article I provide a science-based framework that will help them.

About a decade ago, in an effort to understand how company culture affects performance, I began measuring the brain activity of people while they worked. The neuroscience experiments I have run reveal eight ways that leaders can effectively create and manage a culture of trust. I'll describe those strategies and explain how some organizations are using them to good effect. But first, let's look at the science behind the framework.

What's Happening in the Brain

Back in 2001 I derived a mathematical relationship between trust and economic performance. Though my paper on this research described the social, legal, and economic environments that cause differences in trust, I couldn't answer the most basic question: Why do two people trust each other in the first place? Experiments around the world have shown that humans are naturally inclined to trust others—but don't always. I hypothesized that there must be a neurologic signal that indicates when we should trust someone. So I started a long-term research program to see if that was true.

I knew that in rodents a brain chemical called oxytocin had been shown to signal that another animal was safe to approach. I wondered if that was the case in humans, too. No one had looked into it, so I decided to investigate. To measure trust and its reciprocation (trustworthiness) objectively, my team used a strategic decision task developed by researchers in the lab of Vernon Smith, a Nobel laureate in economics. In our experiment, a participant chooses an amount of money to send to a stranger via computer, knowing that

Idea in Brief

The Problem

Leaders know that low employee engagement is a sign of lost value—it's clearly something they want to fix. But most of them don't know how, so they provide random perks, hoping those will move the needle.

The Solution

It's much more effective to create a culture of trust. Neuroscience research shows that you can do this through eight key management behaviors that stimulate the production of oxytocin, a brain chemical that facilitates teamwork.

The Payoff

By fostering organizational trust, you can increase employees' productivity and energy levels, improve collaboration, and cultivate a happier, more loyal workforce.

the money will triple in amount and understanding that the recipient may or may not share the spoils. Therein lies the conflict: The recipient can either keep all the cash or be trustworthy and share it with the sender.

To measure oxytocin levels during the exchange, my colleagues and I developed a protocol to draw blood from people's arms before and immediately after they made decisions to trust others (if they were senders) or to be trustworthy (if they were receivers). Because we didn't want to influence their behavior, we didn't tell participants what the study was about, even though there was no way they could consciously control how much oxytocin they produced. We found that the more money people received (denoting greater trust on the part of senders), the more oxytocin their brains produced. And the amount of oxytocin recipients produced predicted how trustworthy—that is, how likely to share the money—they would be.

Since the brain generates messaging chemicals all the time, it was possible we had simply observed random changes in oxytocin. To prove that it *causes* trust, we safely administered doses of synthetic oxytocin into living human brains (through a nasal spray). Comparing participants who received a real dose with those who received a placebo, we found that giving people 24 IU of synthetic oxytocin

How Trust Creates Joy

EXPERIMENTS SHOW THAT HAVING A SENSE of higher purpose stimulates oxytocin production, as does trust. Trust and purpose then mutually reinforce each other, providing a mechanism for extended oxytocin release, which produces happiness.

So, joy on the job comes from doing purpose-driven work with a trusted team. In the nationally representative data set described in the main article, the correlation between (1) trust reinforced by purpose and (2) joy is very high: 0.77. It means that joy can be considered a "sufficient statistic" that reveals how effectively your company's culture engages employees. To measure this, simply ask, "How much do you enjoy your job on a typical day?"

more than doubled the amount of money they sent to a stranger. Using a variety of psychological tests, we showed that those receiving oxytocin remained cognitively intact. We also found that they did not take excessive risks in a gambling task, so the increase in trust was not due to neural disinhibition. Oxytocin appeared to do just one thing—reduce the fear of trusting a stranger.

My group then spent the next 10 years running additional experiments to identify the promoters and inhibitors of oxytocin. This research told us why trust varies across individuals and situations. For example, high stress is a potent oxytocin inhibitor. (Most people intuitively know this: When they are stressed out, they do not interact with others effectively.) We also discovered that oxytocin increases a person's empathy, a useful trait for social creatures trying to work together. We were starting to develop insights that could be used to design high-trust cultures, but to confirm them, we had to get out of the lab.

So we obtained permission to run experiments at numerous field sites where we measured oxytocin and stress hormones and then assessed employees' productivity and ability to innovate. This research even took me to the rain forest of Papua New Guinea, where I measured oxytocin in indigenous people to see if the relationship between oxytocin and trust is universal. (It is.) Drawing on all these findings, I created a survey instrument that quantifies trust within organizations by measuring its constituent factors (described in the next section). That survey has allowed me to study several thousand companies and develop a framework for managers.

How to Manage for Trust

Through the experiments and the surveys, I identified eight management behaviors that foster trust. These behaviors are measurable and can be managed to improve performance.

Recognize excellence

The neuroscience shows that recognition has the largest effect on trust when it occurs immediately after a goal has been met, when it comes from peers, and when it's tangible, unexpected, personal, and public. Public recognition not only uses the power of the crowd to celebrate successes but also inspires others to aim for excellence. And it gives top performers a forum for sharing best practices, so others can learn from them.

Barry-Wehmiller Companies, a supplier of manufacturing and technology services, is a high-trust organization that effectively recognizes top performers in the 80 production-automation manufacturers it owns. CEO Bob Chapman and his team started a program in which employees at each plant nominate an outstanding peer annually. The winner is kept secret until announced to everyone, and the facility is closed on the day of the celebration. The chosen employee's family and close friends are invited to attend (without tipping off the winner), and the entire staff joins them. Plant leaders kick off the ceremony by reading the nominating letters about the winner's contributions and bring it to a close with a favorite perk—the keys to a sports car the winner gets to drive for a week. Though the recognition isn't immediate, it is tangible, unexpected, and both personal and public. And by having employees help pick the winners, Barry-Wehmiller gives everyone, not just the people at the top, a say in what constitutes excellence. All this seems to be working well for the company: It has grown from a single plant in 1987 to a conglomerate that brings in $2.4 billion in annual revenue today.

Induce "challenge stress"

When a manager assigns a team a difficult but achievable job, the moderate stress of the task releases neurochemicals, including oxytocin and adrenocorticotropin, that intensify people's focus and strengthen social connections. When team members need to work together to reach a goal, brain activity coordinates their behaviors efficiently. But this works only if challenges are attainable and have a concrete end point; vague or impossible goals cause people to give up before they even start. Leaders should check in frequently to assess progress and adjust goals that are too easy or out of reach.

The need for achievability is reinforced by Harvard Business School professor Teresa Amabile's findings on the power of progress: When Amabile analyzed 12,000 diary entries of employees from a variety of industries, she found that 76% of people reported that their best days involved making progress toward goals.

Give people discretion in how they do their work

Once employees have been trained, allow them, whenever possible, to manage people and execute projects in their own way. Being trusted to figure things out is a big motivator: A 2014 Citigroup and LinkedIn survey found that nearly half of employees would give up a 20% raise for greater control over how they work.

Autonomy also promotes innovation, because different people try different approaches. Oversight and risk management procedures can help minimize negative deviations while people experiment. And postproject debriefs allow teams to share how positive deviations came about so that others can build on their success.

Often, younger or less experienced employees will be your chief innovators, because they're less constrained by what "usually" works. That's how progress was made in self-driving cars. After five years and a significant investment by the U.S. government in the big three auto manufacturers, no autonomous military vehicles had been produced. Changing tack, the Defense Advanced Research Projects Agency offered all comers a large financial prize for a self-driving car that could complete a course in the Mojave Desert in less than 10 hours. Two years later a group of engineering students from Stanford University won the challenge—and $2 million.

Enable job crafting

When companies trust employees to choose which projects they'll work on, people focus their energies on what they care about most. As a result, organizations like the Morning Star Company—the largest producer of tomato products in the world—have highly productive colleagues who stay with the company year after year. At Morning Star (a company I've worked with), people don't even have job titles; they self-organize into work groups. Gaming software company Valve gives employees desks on wheels and encourages them to join projects that seem "interesting" and "rewarding." But they're still held accountable. Clear expectations are set when employees join a new group, and 360-degree evaluations are done when projects wrap up, so that individual contributions can be measured.

Share information broadly

Only 40% of employees report that they are well informed about their company's goals, strategies, and tactics. This uncertainty about the company's direction leads to chronic stress, which inhibits the release of oxytocin and undermines teamwork. Openness is the antidote. Organizations that share their "flight plans" with employees reduce uncertainty about where they are headed and why. Ongoing communication is key: A 2015 study of 2.5 million manager-led teams in 195 countries found that workforce engagement improved when supervisors had some form of daily communication with direct reports.

Social media optimization company Buffer goes further than most by posting its salary formula online for everyone to see. Want to know what CEO Joel Gascoigne makes? Just look it up. That's openness.

Intentionally build relationships

The brain network that oxytocin activates is evolutionarily old. This means that the trust and sociality that oxytocin enables are

The Impact of Trust in Organizations

COMPARED WITH PEOPLE AT LOW-TRUST COMPANIES, people at high-trust companies report 74% less stress, 106% more energy at work, 50% higher productivity, 13% fewer sick days, 76% more engagement, 29% more satisfaction with their lives, and 40% less burnout.

deeply embedded in our nature. Yet at work we often get the message that we should focus on completing tasks, not on making friends. Neuroscience experiments by my lab show that when people intentionally build social ties at work, their performance improves. A Google study similarly found that managers who "express interest in and concern for team members' success and personal well-being" outperform others in the quality and quantity of their work.

Yes, even engineers need to socialize. A study of software engineers in Silicon Valley found that those who connected with others and helped them with their projects not only earned the respect and trust of their peers but were also more productive themselves. You can help people build social connections by sponsoring lunches, after-work parties, and team-building activities. It may sound like forced fun, but when people care about one another, they perform better because they don't want to let their teammates down. Adding a moderate challenge to the mix (white-water rafting counts) will speed up the social-bonding process.

Facilitate whole-person growth

High-trust workplaces help people develop personally as well as professionally. Numerous studies show that acquiring new work skills isn't enough; if you're not growing as a human being, your performance will suffer. High-trust companies adopt a growth mindset when developing talent. Some even find that when managers set clear goals, give employees the autonomy to reach them, and provide consistent feedback, the backward-looking annual performance review is no longer necessary. Instead, managers and direct reports can meet more frequently to focus on professional and personal growth. This is the approach taken by

Accenture and Adobe Systems. Managers can ask questions like, "Am I helping you get your next job?" to probe professional goals. Assessing personal growth includes discussions about work-life integration, family, and time for recreation and reflection. Investing in the whole person has a powerful effect on engagement and retention.

Show vulnerability

Leaders in high-trust workplaces ask for help from colleagues instead of just telling them to do things. My research team has found that this stimulates oxytocin production in others, increasing their trust and cooperation. Asking for help is a sign of a secure leader— one who engages everyone to reach goals. Jim Whitehurst, CEO of open-source software maker Red Hat, has said, "I found that being very open about the things I did not know actually had the opposite effect than I would have thought. It helped me build credibility." Asking for help is effective because it taps into the natural human impulse to cooperate with others.

The Return on Trust

After identifying and measuring the managerial behaviors that sustain trust in organizations, my team and I tested the impact of trust on business performance. We did this in several ways. First, we gathered evidence from a dozen companies that have launched policy changes to raise trust (most were motivated by a slump in their profits or market share). Second, we conducted the field experiments mentioned earlier: In two businesses where trust varies by department, my team gave groups of employees specific tasks, gauged their productivity and innovation in those tasks, and gathered very detailed data—including direct measures of brain activity—showing that trust improves performance. And third, with the help of an independent survey firm, we collected data in February 2016 from a nationally representative sample of 1,095 working adults in the U.S. The findings from all three sources were similar, but I will focus on what we learned from the national data since it's generalizable.

By surveying the employees about the extent to which firms practiced the eight behaviors, we were able to calculate the level of trust for each organization. (To avoid priming respondents, we never used the word "trust" in surveys.) The U.S. average for organizational trust was 70% (out of a possible 100%). Fully 47% of respondents worked in organizations where trust was below the average, with one firm scoring an abysmally low 15%. Overall, companies scored lowest on recognizing excellence and sharing information (67% and 68%, respectively). So the data suggests that the average U.S. company could enhance trust by improving in these two areas—even if it didn't improve in the other six.

The effect of trust on self-reported work performance was powerful. Respondents whose companies were in the top quartile indicated they had 106% more energy and were 76% more engaged at work than respondents whose firms were in the bottom quartile. They also reported being 50% more productive—which is consistent with our objective measures of productivity from studies we have done with employees at work. Trust had a major impact on employee loyalty as well: Compared with employees at low-trust companies, 50% more of those working at high-trust organizations planned to stay with their employer over the next year, and 88% more said they would recommend their company to family and friends as a place to work.

My team also found that those working in high-trust companies enjoyed their jobs 60% more, were 70% more aligned with their companies' purpose, and felt 66% closer to their colleagues. And a high-trust culture improves how people treat one another and themselves. Compared with employees at low-trust organizations, the high-trust folks had 11% more empathy for their workmates, depersonalized them 41% less often, and experienced 40% less burnout from their work. They felt a greater sense of accomplishment, as well—41% more.

Again, this analysis supports the findings from our qualitative and scientific studies. But one new—and surprising—thing we learned is that high-trust companies pay more. Employees earn an additional $6,450 a year, or 17% more, at companies in the highest quartile of trust, compared with those in the lowest quartile. The only way this can occur in a competitive labor market is if employees in high-trust companies are more productive and innovative.

Former Herman Miller CEO Max De Pree once said, "The first responsibility of a leader is to define reality. The last is to say thank you. In between the two, the leader must become a servant."

The experiments I have run strongly support this view. Ultimately, you cultivate trust by setting a clear direction, giving people what they need to see it through, and getting out of their way.

It's not about being easy on your employees or expecting less from them. High-trust companies hold people accountable but without micromanaging them. They treat people like responsible adults.

Originally published in January–February 2017. Reprint R1701E

Dig, Bridge, Collectively Act

by Tina Opie and Beth A. Livingston

WHEN MARGARET MITCHELL, a white woman, asked Timnit Gebru, a Black woman, to join the ethical AI team at Google, Gebru didn't know what to say. Though she was flattered and intrigued, she was aware of Google's lack of racial and gender diversity. Friends had warned her that the environment might prove hostile to a woman of color. In 2018, the year she was hired, Black employees represented only 2.6% of Google's U.S. workforce. But Mitchell convinced Gebru that if they stuck together, they could bring about real change in the organization. Soon after, however, the women say, they both witnessed racist and sexist patterns at the company. In response they reached out individually to people within the firm to push them to think more ethically and equitably. They tried to dig into why these problems existed at Google and to build bridges with colleagues to enact positive change. They claim that their efforts were met with strong opposition by Google executives.

The situation reached a breaking point in 2020. In a message sent to a listserv for women who worked for Google Brain, one of the company's AI labs, Gebru accused the company of "silencing marginalized voices" and referred to Google's internal diversity programs as a waste of time. Gebru says she was fired shortly thereafter. (Google says she resigned.) Next, Mitchell was suspended when Google discovered her searching her own email account for evidence of discrimination against Gebru. Several weeks later Mitchell was fired for "multiple violations of [Google's] code of conduct, as well as of our security policies, which included exfiltration of confidential, business-sensitive documents," Google said in a statement to *TechCrunch*.

The tech giant's alleged treatment of Gebru and Mitchell is representative of the larger problem of gender and racial inequality in business. Women lead just 6% of the top 3,000 public companies in the United States. In the spring of 2022 only 44 of the *Fortune* 500 CEOs were women, and only six were Black (two of whom were women). Only four Black women and 24 Black men have ever been *Fortune* 500 CEOs. The problem permeates the ranks as well. In 2021 women earned 83% of what men earned in the United States, and Black and Latina women earned 63% and 58% of what white men did, respectively.

Movements like #MeToo and Black Lives Matter have highlighted the need for business leaders to publicly commit to combating discrimination and racism. But commitments alone won't dismantle systemic inequities, so we've decided to explore how organizations can create lasting societal change, drawing on our combined four decades of experience researching and advising companies on strategic management and organizational behavior and on the insights gained from our real-life experiences.

In this article we present our solution: the Shared Sisterhood framework, which is based on a set of practices we call Dig, Bridge, and Collectively Act. Shared Sisterhood is designed to achieve organizational and individual equity across genders and racioethnicities. (*Racioethnicity*, a term first used by Taylor Cox in a 1991 article, "The Multicultural Organization," is defined as race and culture, and it encompasses such identities as Black/African American, white, Indigenous/Native American, Hispanic, Asian, Middle Eastern, and multicultural.) We've helped 12 large and midsize companies, in industries ranging from financial services to entertainment to law, implement the Shared Sisterhood approach, and we've seen it have significant impact.

Although Shared Sisterhood was originally intended to examine the challenges faced by both Black and white women in the United

Idea in Brief

The Problem

In the wake of George Floyd's murder, many companies announced commitments to racial equity and diversity. Unfortunately, since then organizational change has not occurred at the level and frequency that initial public responses suggested.

The Cause

Commitments alone will not dismantle systemic inequities. Organizations must help facilitate lasting change.

The Solution

The Shared Sisterhood framework, which is based on the practices of Dig, Bridge, and Collectively Act, is designed to help achieve equity across genders and racioethnicities.

States and offer solutions to connect the two communities, its general principles can be used to strengthen relationships between members of other racioethnic groups (and other kinds of identity groups). In our consulting work we've applied these principles in a variety of workplace conversations among people from varying racioethnic backgrounds. While the experiences of the participants differed, many of them were amazed to discover that they could see themselves in one another. Coming together to talk about their differences helped them better understand how to form authentic connections with people outside their own groups.

Our call to action begins on the individual level, but action has to take place on an organizational level to deliver institutional and societal change. In this article we'll start by examining how and why people should constantly explore their own assumptions, biases, and individual and collective power. We'll then reveal the ways in which people can use their self-exploration to build bridges with colleagues from different racioethnicities and genders. Finally, we'll discuss how those bridges can be used to make professional environments more welcoming and inclusive.

Dig In

Dig is a practice designed to help you surface your assumptions about racioethnicity and understand how they frame your perceptions of the world and influence your interpersonal relationships. Because your assumptions and perceptions may shift as you grow and encounter different people and experience new workplaces and contexts, digging is something you need to do continually. It involves taking the following steps:

Identify who you are

We all have multiple social identities. The first thing you need to do is figure out what yours are and how strongly you connect with each one. In Shared Sisterhood workshops, participants record all this on a worksheet. Someone's identities might include "woman" or "man" or "nonbinary" and "Hispanic" or "Black" or "Chinese." They also might include "Christian" or "southerner" or even "fan of such-and-such sports team."

Research power dynamics

The next step is to try to understand how identities fit into the broader context of history and status. Some identities are imbued with social power (for example, being white, being a man), while some have been historically marginalized (being Black, being a woman). You need to do some homework on the dynamics associated with your identities. To develop your understanding of these dynamics you can read books about gender, race, ethnicity, religion, class, and so on, and consult trusted websites with commentary from scholars and experts who are endorsed by those who share your desire to grow and learn. Works we recommend include *Our Separate Ways: Black and White Women and the Struggle for Professional Identity,* by Ella Bell Smith and Stella Nkomo; *Right Within: How to Heal from Racial Trauma in the Workplace,* by Minda Harts; "A Theory of Racialized Organizations," by Victor Ray; and the podcast *Truth's Table.* Librarians, social scientists, and teachers can provide additional suggestions. (Tip: Start with one well-researched book and then consult the footnotes and end-notes for further reading material.) Remember that many of us simultaneously belong to groups with different levels of status in our society.

Recognize your knowledge gaps

Often, people from privileged groups particularly benefit from educating themselves about the power dynamics related to their groups. However, persistent—or unrecognized—knowledge gaps are almost inevitable. White privilege, for example, may not be apparent to people until they dig into the many ways structural racism benefits white people—even those from lower-income or otherwise marginalized groups. As you do research on your identities, pay attention when questions remain and when your confusion persists. The need to learn is nothing to be ashamed of. A learning orientation can help you focus on the future instead of the past, but it's critical that when you dig up a knowledge gap, you work to close it. Whether you're from a power-dominant or a historically marginalized group, digging will equip you with personal insights that help you successfully build bridges with others.

You also need to understand the common responses to knowledge gaps to make sure that your reaction to them promotes personal growth. For instance, research suggests that white people often have one of three responses to being told about the power and privilege associated with their racial identity: They deny and refute the existence of their power, psychologically detach or distance themselves from their white identity (to show that they "aren't like *those* white people"), or work to eliminate systems of inequity that privilege their group over other racioethnicities.

Bridge Differences

Bridges are built when two people develop authentic connections across their differences—when they can express their thoughts, beliefs, assumptions, ideas, emotions, and so on to each other in a relationship characterized by trust, empathy, vulnerability, and risk-taking. While those four components don't have to be at the same level for both parties, both must be willing to engage in them. It's also important to assess your preparedness to bridge: Where do you stand emotionally and mentally? Are you ready for the hard work of connecting across differences? If you're a member of a power-dominant group, that means honestly confronting historical inequities, listening to and focusing on your coworkers' concerns, and acknowledging and engaging with the authentic emotions of marginalized group members as you discuss equity and inclusion. It means taking a risk to speak up in defense of equity and justice—even when it makes you uncomfortable. It may also mean making yourself vulnerable by letting your guard down to interact with someone new. If you're a member of a historically marginalized group, it's important to assess your willingness to trust members of historically power-dominant groups, who typically have done less self-exploration. Are you able to interact with people who may have more work to do? When you attempt to bridge and become frustrated, how will you take care of yourself? How will you know if it is safe for you to try to bridge with those people again?

Each time a pair of individuals connect authentically at work, they put down one layer of a bridge. The more they connect, the stronger the bridge grows. Once a bridge is built, both people can reach out to others to develop more bridges, which then serve as channels for collective action on equity.

In practice, bridges between people of different racioethnicities may be difficult to build if the parties are unable or unwilling to discuss racism. But that does not mean that every bridge interaction must be centered on racioethnicity or racism. Once people establish that they hold similar values—perhaps through joint attendance at diversity and equity events at work—they might need to develop trust by talking about things besides racism, especially at the beginning of the process. But they shouldn't avoid the topic. Demonstrating one's trustworthiness and shared values around equity is critical. Authenticity is key to the success of such conversations;

empty platitudes and virtue signaling will backfire. That is why digging before bridging is so important.

One woman we worked with, whom we'll call Sarah, was charged with improving gender equity at her male-dominated firm. Women in leadership were few and far between. As Sarah observed the disparities in race and gender at the executive level, she realized that she didn't have deep knowledge about how to combat racism. She wanted to learn how to take an intersectional approach so that she could address both gender and racioethnic inequities. She reached out to her Black, Asian, and Hispanic female colleagues to learn more. During those interactions, Sarah—who's white—first focused on herself, digging to understand her own assumptions around race and equity. She began to unearth her blind spots—recognizing, for instance, that she may have lumped all women into one category, failing to see that the intersection of race and gender can lead to vastly different workplace experiences. Then she looked for colleagues who were different from her but who shared her values. She chatted with them about things that really mattered to her—job-related issues, issues in the news that they both cared about (concerning sports or politics), or anything else she thought her colleagues would be receptive to and that would demonstrate her willingness to connect. She didn't force the relationships but found authentic ways to build them. Over time the bridges she created grew stronger as Sarah proactively demonstrated her vulnerability and deepened trust by first looking inward when she and her coworkers faced issues of conflict, such as what to emphasize (gender, race, or both) when presenting diversity, equity, and inclusion concerns to senior executives. These connections paved the way to increasing the number of women in the leadership pipeline, particularly women of color—all of whom she supported and elevated. Sarah could have focused solely on gender equity and overlooked racioethnic equity, but she integrated the two and created deeper change.

While authentic connections are critical building blocks, they're not the end goal. They form the foundation of bridges across differences, which become catalysts for progress on organizational and societal racial and gender equity.

Act Collectively for Positive Change

Each individual action toward equity can beget opportunities for additional connections and actions, until you have generated a latticework of connections that are primed to dismantle systemic inequities. A critical mass of people who have bridged together can exert power and pressure the organization to change. No one person will be responsible for the movement; the group will coordinate efforts and determine who is best positioned to say what, when, and to whom.

To effectively mobilize together, however, people from different groups all must first perceive that there is discrimination to fight or a problem to solve. Increasing awareness of current inequity and injustice is a critical step in moving toward change. That's again why digging is so important.

Ava DuVernay's efforts on the set of the TV show *Queen Sugar* represent a true application of the Shared Sisterhood framework. DuVernay has won wide acclaim—including Golden Globe, Oscar, and Emmy nominations—for her work presenting the lives of fully realized Black characters.

DuVernay got her opportunity in television from two trailblazing Black women. The acclaimed showrunner Shonda Rhimes gave DuVernay her first shot in TV, inviting her to direct an episode of *Scandal.* Then, Oprah Winfrey provided her with a platform (on the Oprah Winfrey Network) to launch her own show, *Queen Sugar,* which Winfrey executive produces. At the time, DuVernay was one of the few female directors of color: Women directed only 17% of American TV shows, with only 3% directed by women from historically marginalized groups. Women often faced exhortations to "get more experience" to direct and write in Hollywood, but few gave them the chance to do so.

DuVernay wasn't content to be one of the few who "made it." She announced that she was going to uplift other women by hiring only female directors, focusing particularly on those of color, to work on *Queen Sugar.* The effect was swift. Soon the writers' room was majority female, and most key positions were held by women.

DuVernay and her diverse team created systems that provided less-experienced people with the right resources and knowledge, such as a guidebook of information on how the show ran logistically and creatively. "We understand that everyone coming in hasn't done this before," DuVernay's showrunner, Kat Candler, told *The Lily*. "Everybody knows that we're educating through this process. There's a safety net, a support group." The show has turned into something of a talent pipeline, according to the *Hollywood Reporter;* several novice directors have gotten jobs with other TV series because of their work on *Queen Sugar*.

One Firm's Experience

Collective action doesn't always start at the individual level. In the summer of 2020 one advisory firm's leadership team began using our framework to address concerns about the impact that traumatic racial events, including George Floyd's killing, were having on employees. The company's senior leadership team wanted to connect with employees across different racioethnic backgrounds better, promote equity within the organization, and help identify and address microaggressions as they occurred. (Microaggressions are commonplace instances of what Derald Sue of Columbia University calls "verbal, behavioral, or environmental indignities, whether intentional or unintentional, that communicate hostile, derogatory, or negative . . . slights and insults" to people from marginalized groups. Examples include assuming that a female physician wearing a stethoscope is a nurse and clutching one's purse when passing a Black or Latino man on the street.)

The project included a four-month series of immersive training workshops and small peer-group sessions overseen by an external diversity, equity, and inclusion expert. Although we're not allowed to describe in detail what happened during the workshops, with clients we take an approach very much like the one we outlined earlier: We encourage participants to record their identities on worksheets. With members of historically power-dominant groups, we ask what other groups have been marginalized by their group, and how and why. We ask them to think about the ways members of their group have benefited from and perpetuated the power dynamics they experience today—individually, socially, and institutionally. People are often resistant to this question. ("My identity has never benefited me. I've had to work hard for everything I've gotten" is a response we often hear.) When we see this, we push people to ask questions such as "In what specific ways has my identity given me advantages—for instance, access, connections, or resources—that others don't have? In what specific ways have others with different identities been disadvantaged—for instance, by barriers that I don't face?" With members of historically marginalized groups, we ask what other groups have been privileged by their group's lack of power—and how and why—again on an individual, social, and institutional level.

The second phase of the firm's workshops focused on bridging differences between the leaders so that they could understand how microaggressions affected others. At workshops like these we typically start by presenting a mini case study, such as an example of a microaggression that occurs at workplaces—like complimenting an Asian American colleague on his English (as if he were not a "true" American). We then ask participants a series of questions to explore how people from different backgrounds interpret the microaggression, what leads someone to commit it, and how it makes the person on the receiving end feel. Then the group talks about what can be done to correct the problem.

This work helps participants improve their ability to connect authentically with people who are different from them. Understanding what others are thinking, feeling, and doing is a critical step. The next step—identifying what inspires those thoughts, feelings, and actions—is equally important. The goal is not to assign blame or excuse behavior—it is simply to understand the reasons people respond the way they do. And ideally, participants from dominant groups will then fully recognize injustices and agree that something needs to be done about them. Real collective action won't happen until they do.

Successful collective efforts might start when one member of a bridge pursues equity for an entire organization; when two partners from different racioethnic groups work side by side as a united front; or when many partners in a larger group, such as a firm's leadership team, do what they can to move their organization toward fairer, more-just practices.

The advisory firm's workshops culminated in a focus on collective action and how the leadership team could make the organization more equitable. At this stage all parties must agree to prioritize reducing inequity over their individual comfort or goals. The firm decided to develop an e-learning platform to provide ongoing diversity, equity, and inclusion training for all employees. Moreover, when a national racial tragedy occurs now, members of the leadership team pitch in to help draft firmwide communications, a task previously left to the communications function. The firm is also doing a pay-equity analysis that it plans to release by mid-2023. Perhaps most encouraging: Each member of the leadership team now conducts his or her own workshops on equity for direct reports and other managers within the company. In doing so, the leaders ensure that the Dig, Bridge, and Collectively Act process continues indefinitely throughout the organization's ranks.

———————

The actions of Gebru and Mitchell, who bravely banded together when they saw people in their organization treated unfairly, put public pressure on Google and other technology companies to improve their responses to inequity. After both women had moved on from Google, their manager, a strong supporter of theirs who said he was stunned by how they'd been treated, quit. On Twitter, Gebru and Mitchell's influence continues. They often discuss how they navigated discrimination at Google by standing up for each other and fighting their treatment together. Gebru has launched a new organization, the Distributed AI Research Institute, where she has continued her work on equity and ethics in technology. Two members of Gebru's old Google team, Alex Hanna and Dylan Baker, followed Gebru to her new firm, demonstrating how professional bridges can span organizational boundaries and help people recover from setbacks.

Only by digging into our identities and the power structures that surround them can we begin to build bridges with people from different backgrounds and then work with those people to act together. This often happens on an interpersonal level, but it's critical that companies also take institutional steps to ensure healthy and productive environments for all employees. Companies are frequently bold in their innovations for products, services, and strategies. Being bold in the service of equity is a necessity as well.

Originally published in September–October 2022. Reprint R2205E

Rethinking Trust

by Roderick M. Kramer

FOR THE PAST TWO DECADES, trust has been touted as the all-powerful lubricant that keeps the economic wheels turning and greases the right connections—all to our collective benefit. Popular business books proclaim the power and virtue of trust. Academics have enthusiastically piled up study after study showing the varied benefits of trust, especially when it is based on a clear track record, credible expertise, and prominence in the right networks.

Then along came Bernie. There was "something about this person, pedigree, and reputation that inspired trust," mused one broker taken in by Bernard Madoff, who confessed to a $65 billion Ponzi scheme—one of the largest and most successful in history. On the surface, Madoff possessed all the bona fides—the record, the résumé, the expertise, and the social connections. But the fact that so many people, including some sophisticated financial experts and business leaders, were lulled into a false sense of security when dealing with Madoff should give us pause. Why are we so prone to trusting?

Madoff is hardly the first to pull the wool over so many eyes. What about Enron, WorldCom, Tyco, and all the other corporate scandals of the past decade? Is there perhaps a problem with how we trust?

I have been grappling with this question for most of my 30 years as a social psychologist, exploring both the strengths and the weaknesses of trust. In the wake of the recent massive and pervasive abuses—and with evidence of more scandals surfacing each day—I think it's worth taking another look at why we trust so readily, why we sometimes trust poorly, and what we can do about it.

In the following pages, I present the thesis that human beings are naturally predisposed to trust—it's in our genes and our childhood learning—and by and large it's a survival mechanism that has served our species well. That said, our willingness to trust often gets us into trouble. Moreover, we sometimes have difficulty distinguishing trustworthy people from untrustworthy ones. At a species level, that doesn't matter very much so long as more people are trustworthy than not. At the individual level, though, it can be a real problem. To survive as individuals, we'll have to learn to trust wisely and well. That kind of trust—I call it *tempered trust*—doesn't come easily, but if you diligently ask yourself the right questions, you can develop it.

Let's begin by looking at why we're so prone to trust.

To Trust Is Human

It all starts with the brain. Thanks to our large brains, humans are born physically premature and highly dependent on caretakers. Because of this need, we enter the world "hardwired" to make social connections. The evidence is impressive: Within *one hour* of birth, a human infant will draw her head back to look into the eyes and face of the person gazing at her. Within a few more hours, the infant will orient her head in the direction of her mother's voice. And, unbelievable as it may seem, it's only a matter of hours before the infant can actually mimic a caretaker's expressions. A baby's mother, in turn, responds and mimics her child's expression and emotions within seconds.

In short, we're social beings from the get-go: We're born to be engaged and to engage others, which is what trust is largely about. That has been an advantage in our struggle for survival. As social psychologist Shelley Taylor noted in her summary of the scientific evidence, "Scientists now consider the nurturant qualities of life—the parent-child bond, cooperation, and other benign social ties—to be critical attributes that drove brain development . . . accounting for our success as a species." The tendency to trust made sense in our evolutionary history.

Research has shown that the brain chemistry governing our emotions also plays a role in trust. Paul Zak, a researcher on the cutting

Idea in Brief

Trust is essential for business and economic success. But recent financial scandals suggest that people aren't always very smart about whom they trust. Bernard Madoff took in some of the world's cleverest people.

In evolution, trust served humans well because it increased the chances that vulnerable infants would survive. Our body chemistry rewards us for trusting, and we quickly decide to trust others on the basis of simple surface cues such as their physical similarity to us.

Our readiness to trust makes us likely to make mistakes. At a species level, that doesn't matter so long as more people are trustworthy than not. At the individual level, though, misplaced trust can get us into trouble. To survive as individuals, we'll have to learn to temper our trust.

edge of the new field of neuroeconomics, has demonstrated, for instance, that oxytocin, a powerful natural chemical found in our bodies (which plays a role in a mother's labor and milk production) can boost both trust and trustworthiness between people playing experimental trust games. (Even a squirt of oxytocin-laden nasal spray is enough to do it.) Other research has also shown how intimately oxytocin is connected with positive emotional states and the creation of social connections. It's well documented that animals become calmer, more sedate, and less anxious when injected with oxytocin.

Trust kicks in on remarkably simple cues. We're far more likely, for example, to trust people who are similar to us in some dimension. Perhaps the most compelling evidence of this comes from a study by researcher Lisa DeBruine. She developed a clever technique for creating an image of another person that could be morphed to look more and more (or less and less) like a study participant's face. The greater the similarity, DeBruine found, the more the participant trusted the person in the image. This tendency to trust people who resemble us may be rooted in the possibility that such people might be related to us. Other studies have shown that we like and trust people who are members of our own social group more than we like outsiders or strangers. This in-group effect is so powerful that even random assignment into small groups is sufficient to create a sense of solidarity.

As psychologist Dacher Keltner and others have shown, physical touch also has a strong connection to the experience of trust. In one experiment involving a game widely used to study decisions to trust, an experimenter made it a point, while describing the task, to ever so lightly touch the backs of individuals as they were about to play the game. People who received a quick and unobtrusive touch were more likely to cooperate with, rather than compete against, their partner. It's no coincidence, Keltner noted, that greeting rituals throughout the world involve touching—witness the firm, all-American handshake.

So what does all this research add up to? It shows that it often doesn't take much to tip us toward trust. People may say they don't have a lot of trust in others, but their behavior tells a very different story. In fact, in many ways, trust is our default position; we trust routinely, reflexively, and somewhat mindlessly across a broad range of social situations. As clinical psychologist Doris Brothers succinctly put it, "Trust rarely occupies the foreground of conscious awareness. We are no more likely to ask ourselves how trusting we are at any given moment than to inquire if gravity is still keeping the planets in orbit." I call this tendency *presumptive trust* to capture the idea that we approach many situations without any suspicion. Much of the time this predisposition serves us well. Unless we've been unfortunate enough to be victims of a major violation of trust, most of us have had years of experiences that affirm the basic trustworthiness of the people and institutions around us by the time we become adults. Things seldom go catastrophically wrong when we trust, so it's not entirely irrational that we have a bias toward trust.

But Our Judgment Is Sometimes Poor

If it's human to trust, perhaps it's just as human to err. Indeed, a lot of research confirms it. Our exquisitely adapted, cue-driven brains may help us forge trust connections in the first place, but they also make us vulnerable to exploitation. In particular, our tendency to judge trustworthiness on the basis of physical similarities and other surface cues can prove disastrous when combined with the way we process information.

One tendency that skews our judgment is our proclivity to see what we want to see. Psychologists call this the *confirmation bias.* Because of it we pay more attention to, and overweight in importance, evidence supporting our hypotheses about the world, while downplaying or discounting discrepancies or evidence to the contrary. In one laboratory game I conducted, individuals who were primed to expect a possible abuse of trust looked more carefully for signs of untrustworthy behavior from prospective partners. In contrast, those primed with more positive social expectations paid more attention to evidence of others' trustworthiness. Most important, individuals' subsequent decisions about how much to trust the prospective partners were swayed by those expectations.

A confirmation bias wouldn't be so bad if we weren't heavily influenced by the social stereotypes that most of us carry around in our heads. These stereotypes reflect (often false) beliefs that correlate observable cues (facial characteristics, age, gender, race, and so on) with underlying psychological traits (honesty, reliability, likability, or trustworthiness). Psychologists call these beliefs *implicit theories,* and the evidence is overwhelming that we aren't conscious of how they affect our judgment. Most of the time our implicit personality theories are pretty harmless; they simply help us categorize people more quickly and render social judgments more swiftly. But they can cause us to overestimate someone's trustworthiness in situations where a lot is at stake (for instance, our physical safety or financial security).

To make matters worse, people tend to think their own judgment is better than average—including their judgment about whom to trust. In a negotiation class I teach, I routinely find that about 95% of MBA students place themselves in the upper *half* of the distribution when it comes to their ability to "size up" other people accurately, including how trustworthy, reliable, honest, and fair their classmates are. In fact, more than 77% of my students put themselves in the top 25% of their class, and about 20% put themselves in the top 10%. This inflated sense of our own judgment makes us vulnerable to people who can fake outward signs of trustworthiness.

It's not just biases inside our heads that skew our judgment. We often rely on trusted third parties to verify the character or reliability of other people. These third parties, in effect, help us "roll over" our positive expectations from one known and trusted party to another who is less known and trusted. In such situations, trust becomes, quite literally, transitive. Unfortunately, as the Bernie Madoff case illustrates, transitive trust can lull people into a false sense of security. The evidence suggests that Madoff was a master at cultivating and exploiting social connections. One of his hunting grounds was the Orthodox Jewish community, a tight-knit social group.

The biases described thus far contribute to errors in deciding whom to trust. Unfortunately, the wiring in our brains can also hinder our ability to make good decisions about how much risk to assume in our relationships. In particular, researchers have identified two cognitive illusions that increase our propensity to trust too readily, too much, and for too long.

The first illusion causes us to underestimate the likelihood that bad things will happen to us. Research on this *illusion of personal invulnerability* has demonstrated that we think we're not very likely to experience some of life's misfortunes, even though we realize objectively that such risk exists. Thus, although we know intellectually that street crime is a major problem in most cities, we underestimate the chances that we will become victims of it. One reason for this illusion, it's been argued, is the ease with which we engage in a kind of compensatory calculus and call up from memory all the steps we've taken to mitigate such risks (for instance, avoiding dark alleys or making it a habit to cross the street when we see an ominous stranger approaching). The second and closely related illusion is *unrealistic optimism*. Numerous studies have shown that people often overestimate the likelihood that good things will happen to them—that they will marry well, have a successful career, live a long life, and so on. Even when people are given accurate information regarding the true odds of such outcomes, they still tend to think they will do better than average.

As if all these biases and illusions weren't enough, we also have to contend with the fact that the very simplicity of our trust cues leaves us vulnerable to abuse. Unfortunately for us, virtually any indicator of trustworthiness can be manipulated or faked. A number of studies indicate that detecting the cheaters among us is not as easy as one might think. I have been studying deceptive behavior in my lab experiments—and teach about it in my business school courses on power and negotiation. In one exercise, I instruct some participants to do everything they can to "fake" trustworthiness during an upcoming negotiation exercise. I tell them to draw freely on all their intuitive theories regarding behaviors that signal trustworthiness. So what do these short-term sociopaths say and do? Usually, they make it a point to smile a lot; to maintain strong eye contact; to occasionally touch the other person's hand or arm gently. (Women mention touching as a strategy more than men do and, in their post-exercise debriefs, also report using it more than men do.) They engage in cheery banter to relax the other person, and they feign openness during their actual negotiation by saying things like "Let's agree to be honest and we can probably do better at this exercise" and "I always like to put all my cards on the table."

Their efforts turn out to be pretty successful. Most find it fairly easy to get the other person to think they are behaving in a trustworthy, open, cooperative fashion (according to their negotiation partners' ratings of these traits). Additionally, even when students on the other side of the bargaining table were (secretly) forewarned that half the students they might encounter had been instructed to try to fool them and take advantage of them, their ability to detect fakers did not improve: They didn't identify fakers any more accurately than a coin flip would have. Perhaps most interesting, those who had been forewarned actually *felt* they'd done a better job of detecting fakery than did the other students.

We've seen why we trust and also why we sometimes trust poorly. Now it's time to consider how to get trust back on track. If we are to harvest its genuine benefits, we need to trust more prudently.

Temper Your Trust

We can never be certain of another's motivations, intentions, character, or future actions. We simply have to choose between trust (opening ourselves to the prospect of abuse if we're dealing with an exploiter) or distrust (which means missing out on all the benefits if the other person happens to be honest). The shadow of doubt lingers over every decision to trust. That said, there is much that you can do to reduce the doubt—in particular, by adjusting your mind-set and behavioral habits. Here are some preliminary rules for tempering trust.

Rule 1: Know yourself

People generally fall into one of two buckets when it comes to their disposition toward trust. Some trust too much and too readily. They tend to take an overly rosy view, assuming that most people are decent and would never harm them. Thus they disclose personal secrets too early in relationships or share sensitive information in the workplace too indiscriminately, before prudent, incremental foundations of trust have been laid. They talk too freely about their beliefs and impressions of others, without determining whether the person they're conversing with is a friend or a foe. Their overly trusting behavior sets them up for potential grief. In the other bucket are people who are too mistrustful when venturing into relationships. They assume the worst about other people's motivations, intentions, and future actions and thus hold back, avoiding disclosing anything about themselves that might help create a social connection. They're reluctant to reciprocate fully because they fear they'll trust the wrong people. They may make fewer mistakes than their more trusting counterparts do, but they have fewer positive experiences because they keep others at a distance.

The first rule, therefore, is to figure out which of the buckets you fall into, because that will determine what you need to work on. If you're good at trusting but are prone to trust the wrong people, you must get better at interpreting the cues that you receive. If you're good at recognizing cues but have difficulty forging trusting relationships, then you'll have to expand your repertoire of behaviors.

Rule 2: Start small

Trust entails risk. There's no way to avoid that. But you can keep the risks sensible—and sensible means *small,* especially in the early phases of a relationship. Social psychologist David Messick and I coined the term *shallow trust* to describe the kinds of small but productive behaviors through which we can communicate our own willingness to trust.

A good example of this is a gesture made by Hewlett-Packard in the 1980s. HP's management allowed engineers to take equipment home whenever they needed to, including weekends, without having to go through a lot of formal paperwork or red tape. That sent a strong message that the employees taking it off-site could be trusted. The fact that the equipment was subsequently returned validated that trust and, over time, cemented it. Imaginative acts of trust of this sort breed trustworthiness in return. They don't involve much risk, but they broadcast that you're willing to meet people halfway.

Salting your world with lots of small trusting acts sends a signal to others who are themselves interested in building good relationships, and decades of research by social psychologist Svenn Lindskold and others have proved that it leads to more positive interactions. It works because it's incremental (and thus manages the risks intelligently) and contingent (that is, tied to reciprocity). By taking turns with gradually increasing risks, you build a strong and tempered trust with the other person.

Rule 3: Write an escape clause

In our study of trust dynamics in high-stakes situations, Debra Meyerson, Karl Weick, and I found that if people have a clearly articulated plan for disengagement, they can engage more fully and with more commitment. Hedging one's bets in this way may seem as if it would undermine rather than reinforce trust. (After all, how can you expect me to trust you completely if I know you don't trust me completely?) Yet, paradoxically, hedges allow everyone in an organization to trust more easily and comfortably—and even to take larger risks. Because I know your dependence on me is hedged a bit (you have a good backup plan), I have more breathing room as well. All of us know the system will survive the occasional, unavoidable mistakes that permeate any complex organization or social system.

A study I did of novice screenwriters trying to break into the entertainment industry, a domain where betrayals of trust are commonplace, provides a good example of how this works. To get a chance to develop their original ideas for movies or television shows, screenwriters first have to pitch them to agents, independent producers, and studio executives. Once they've done so, however, their ideas are out there—and always at risk of being stolen. (And it's a real prospect: No less a writer than Art Buchwald had this experience when pitching an idea for a movie about an African prince visiting America—an idea that suddenly showed up on the screen a few years later as *Coming to America,* with Eddie Murphy in the starring role. In 1988, Buchwald sued Paramount, claiming the idea was his, and won.) One way to hedge the risk is to write up the treatment and register it first with the Writers Guild of America, which prevents others from claiming it as their own. A second important hedge in Hollywood is to have an agent who can pitch the idea so widely that its authorship becomes well-known. Hollywood is a small world, and making something *common knowledge* in a small world is a good hedging strategy.

Rule 4: Send strong signals

To ensure that trust builds from small initial acts to deeper and broader commitments, it's important to send loud, clear, and consistent signals. Some of the social signals we send are too subtle, though we don't realize it. In one study I did exploring perceptions of reciprocal trust, I found that both managers and subordinates overestimated how much they were trusted by the people in the other category. This discrepancy in self-other perception—a trust gap—has an important implication: Most of us tend to underinvest in communicating our trustworthiness to others, because we take it for granted that they know or can readily discern our wonderful qualities of fairness, honesty, and integrity.

Sending strong and clear signals not only attracts other tempered trusters but also deters potential predators, who are on the lookout for *easy* victims sending weak and inconsistent cues. That's why having a reputation for toughness is critical; reputation is among the most powerful ways we communicate who we are and what kinds of relationships we seek. Robert Axelrod, a pioneer in this stream of research, used the colorful term *provocability* to capture this idea: In order to keep your trust relations on an even keel, and the playing field level, you have to be willing not only to take chances by initially trusting a bit (signaling the willingness to cooperate) but also to retaliate strongly, quickly, and proportionately (signaling that you will strike back when your trust is abused). His research showed that you can be nice and not finish last—but only if you are firm and consistent with respect to punishing offenses.

Rule 5: Recognize the other person's dilemma
It's easy for our self-absorbed brains to fall into the trap of thinking only from our own point of view: After all, it's our own trust dilemmas that we find so anxiety provoking and attention getting. (Whom should I invest my money with? Whom should I allow to operate on me?) We often forget that the people we're dealing with confront their own trust dilemmas and need reassurance when wondering whether (or how much) they should trust us. Some of the best trust builders I've studied display great attention to, and empathy for, the perspective of the other party. They are good mind readers, know what steps to take to reassure people, and proactively allay the anxiety and concerns of others.

A good example is President John F. Kennedy in his famous commencement address at American University in 1963, in which he praised the admirable qualities of the Soviet people and declared his willingness to work toward mutual nuclear disarmament with Soviet leaders. We know from Soviet memoirs that Premier Nikita Khrushchev was impressed, believing that Kennedy was sincere in trying to break from the past and could be trusted to work on this issue.

Rule 6: Look at roles as well as people
Many studies highlight the central importance of personal connections in the trust-building process—and appropriately so. This

finding does not necessarily mean, however, that your trust in leaders or persons of power must be based on a history of sustained personal contact. Research that Debra Meyerson, Karl Weick, and I did on what we call *swift trust* showed that high levels of trust often come from very depersonalized interactions; in fact, personal relations sometimes get in the way of trust.

An important element of swift trust is the presence of clear and compelling roles. Deep trust in a role, we found, can be a substitute for personal experience with an individual. Role-based trust is trust in the system that selects and trains the individual. Robyn Dawes, a psychologist who specializes in human judgment, once observed, "We trust engineers because we trust engineering and that engineers [as individuals] have been taught to apply valid principles of engineering." Thus, the role is a proxy for personal experience and guarantees expertise and motivation—in short, trustworthiness.

Of course, role-based trust isn't foolproof. People on Main Street trusted people on Wall Street for a long time precisely because the U.S. financial system seemed to be producing reliable results that were the envy of the rest of the world. But flawed or not, in deciding whom to trust we still need to take the roles people play into account.

Rule 7: Remain vigilant and always question

When we're hungry, we think about food until we've satisfied our hunger; then our minds move on to the next task confronting us. Human beings seek closure—and that's true of our decisions in trust dilemmas as well. We worry about the trustworthiness of a prospective financial adviser, so we do our due diligence. Once we've made a decision, however, we tend not to revisit it so long as nothing seems to have changed. That's dangerous.

In analyzing accounts of formative trust experiences, I've found that people whose trust was abused were often in situations where they discovered—too late—that the landscape had changed, but they failed to notice because they thought they had already long ago figured out the situation. Despite the fact that a boss's attitude toward them had shifted or someone in the organization was poisoning their reputation, they were living with a false sense of security. They let their vigilance lapse.

The Madoff scandal is a good example. Many people who invested their life savings with Bernie Madoff initially did their due diligence. But once they'd made their decision, their attention turned elsewhere. They were too busy making their money to manage it—which they often didn't feel comfortable doing anyway, because they didn't think of themselves as financial experts. As Holocaust survivor and Nobel Peace Prize winner Elie Wiesel, one of Madoff's many victims, stated, "We checked the people who have business with him, and they were among the best minds on Wall Street, the geniuses of finance. I teach philosophy and literature—and so it happened."

The challenge in revisiting trust is that it requires questioning the people we trust, which is psychologically uncomfortable. But when it comes to situations in which our physical, mental, or financial security is on the line, our trust must be tempered by a sustained, disciplined ambivalence.

Our predisposition to trust has been an important survival skill for young children and, indeed, for us as a species. Recent evidence, moreover, shows that trust plays a critical role in the economic and social vitality of nations, further affirming its fundamental value. But what helps humanity survive doesn't always help the human, and our propensity to trust makes us vulnerable as individuals. To safely reap the full benefits of trust, therefore, we must learn to temper it.

The seven rules I offer here by no means represent a complete primer on how to trust judiciously. The science of trust is also much less complete than we would like, although it is growing rapidly as neuroeconomists, behavioral economists, and psychologists use powerful new techniques such as brain imaging and agent modeling to discover more about how we make judgments about whom to trust and when. But for all their shortcomings, these rules will help you make a good start on what will be a lifelong process of learning how to trust wisely and well.

Originally published in June 2009. Reprint R0906H

How to Negotiate with a Liar

by Leslie K. John

ROBUST SOCIAL PSYCHOLOGY RESEARCH indicates that people lie—and lie often. One prominent study found that people tell, on average, one or two lies every day. Negotiators are no exception. Judging from studies done in 1999 and 2005, roughly half of those making deals will lie when they have a motive and the opportunity to do so. Typically they see it as a way to gain the upper hand (although it can actually cause backlash and prevent the kind of creative problem solving that leads to win-win deals). Deception is thus one of the intangibles that negotiators have to prepare for and take steps to prevent.

Many people assume that the solution is to get better at detecting deception. There's a widespread notion that one can reliably spot a liar through subtle behavioral cues—or "tells," in the parlance of poker and other games that involve bluffing. But the evidence doesn't support that belief. One meta-analysis (a study of studies) found that people can correctly identify whether someone is telling a lie only 54% of the time—not much better odds than a coin flip. Even the polygraph—a technology specifically engineered to detect lies in a controlled setting—is riddled with problems and comes to the wrong conclusion about a third of the time. Humans are particularly inept at recognizing lies that are cloaked in flattery: your boss's promise that a promotion is coming any day now; the supplier's assurance that your order is his top priority. We're wired to readily accept information that conforms to our preexisting assumptions or hopes.

Is there anything you can do to ensure you're not duped in a negotiation? Yes, if you focus on prevention rather than detection. There are several science-backed strategies that can help you conduct conversations in a way that makes it more difficult for your counterpart to lie. Though these methods aren't fail-safe, they will leave you better positioned in your deal making and help you to create maximum value.

1. Encourage Reciprocity

Humans have a strong inclination to reciprocate disclosure: When someone shares sensitive information with us, our instinct is to match their transparency. In fact, simply telling people that others—even strangers—have divulged secrets encourages reciprocation. In a series of studies that I conducted with Alessandro Acquisti and George Loewenstein, we presented readers of the *New York Times* with a list of unethical behaviors, such as making a false insurance claim and cheating on one's tax return. People who were told that "most other participants" had admitted doing those things were 27% more likely to reveal that they had done likewise than were people who were told that only a few others had made such admissions.

Reciprocity is particularly pronounced in face-to-face interactions. In experiments led separately by Arthur Aron and Constantine Sedikides, randomly paired participants who worked their way through a series of questions designed to elicit mutual self-disclosure were more likely to become friends than were pairs instructed to simply make small talk. (One couple assigned to the disclosure exercise eventually married!) Inducing a close relationship is not the primary goal of most negotiations, of course. But other research, by Maurice Schweitzer and Rachel Croson, shows that people lie less to those they know and trust than they do to strangers.

A good way to jump-start reciprocity is to be the first to disclose on an issue of strategic importance (because your counterpart is likely to share information in the same category). For example, imagine you are selling a piece of land. The price it will command depends on how it's developed. So you might tell a potential buyer that you want to sell the land for the best use. This could prompt her to divulge her plans; at a minimum, you are encouraging a conversation about interests, which is critical to creating mutually beneficial deals. This strategy has the added benefit of letting you frame the negotiation, which can enhance your chances of finding breakthroughs.

2. Ask the Right Questions

Most people like to think of themselves as honest. Yet many negotiators guard sensitive information that could undermine their competitive position. In other words, they lie by omission, failing to volunteer pertinent facts. For example, consider an individual who is selling his business but knows that vital equipment needs replacing—a problem imperceptible to outsiders. It might seem unethical for him to withhold that information, but he may feel that by simply avoiding the topic, he can charge a higher price while still maintaining his integrity. "If the buyer had asked me, I would have told the truth!" he might insist.

The risk of not getting the whole story is why it's so important to test your negotiating partners with direct questions. Schweitzer and Croson found that 61% of negotiators came clean when asked about information that weakened their bargaining power, compared to 0% of those not asked. Unfortunately, this tactic can backfire. In the same experiment, 39% of negotiators who were questioned about the information ultimately lied. But you can go a long way toward avoiding that outcome by posing your queries carefully. Research by Julia Minson, Nicole Ruedy, and Schweitzer indicates that people are less likely to lie if questioners make pessimistic assumptions ("This business will need some new equipment soon, right?") rather than optimistic ones ("The equipment is in good order, right?"). It seems to be easier for people to lie by affirming an untrue statement than by negating a true statement.

3. Watch for Dodging

Savvy counterparts often get around direct questions by answering not what they were asked but what they *wish* they'd been asked. And, unfortunately, we are not naturally gifted at detecting this sort of evasiveness. As Todd Rogers and Michael Norton have found, listeners usually don't notice dodges, often because they've forgotten what they originally asked. In fact, the researchers discovered that people are more impressed by eloquent sidestepping than by answers that are relevant but inarticulate.

Dodge detection is improved, however, when listeners are prompted to remember the question—for example, when it is visible as the speaker replies. In a negotiation, therefore, it's a good idea to come to the table with a list of questions, leaving space to jot down your counterpart's answers. Take time after each response to consider whether it actually provided the information you sought. Only when the answer to *that* question is "yes" should you move on to the next issue.

4. Don't Dwell on Confidentiality

Research shows that when we work to assure others that we'll maintain their privacy and confidentiality, we may actually raise their suspicions, causing them to clam up and share less. As early as the 1970s, the National Research Council documented this paradox with potential survey participants: The greater the promises of protection, the less willing people were to respond. This relationship holds up in experimental research. In studies conducted by Eleanor Singer, Hans-Jürgen Hippler, and Norbert Schwarz, for example, fewer than half of the people who received a strong confidentiality assurance agreed to complete an innocuous survey, whereas about 75% of those given no such assurance agreed to do so.

My colleagues and I have discovered that strong privacy protections can also increase lying. In addition, we've found that when questions are posed in a casual tone rather than a formal one, people are more likely to divulge sensitive information. Imagine you are negotiating a job offer with a prospective employee and would like to assess the strength of her other options: Does she have competitive offers? She's likely to be more forthcoming if you avoid or at least minimize confidentiality assurances and instead nonchalantly broach the topic: "We all know there are tons of great firms out there. Any chance you might be considering other places?" Of course, you should still properly protect any confidential information you receive, but there's no reason to announce that unless asked.

5. Cultivate Leaks

People inadvertently leak information in all kinds of ways, including in their own questions. For example, suppose you are in charge of procurement for a firm and you're about to sign a contract with a supplier who has promised to deliver goods within six months. Before signing, he asks you what happens in the event of late delivery. The question could be innocent, but it might also signal his worries about meeting the schedule. So you need to pay attention.

When people leak mindlessly, the information tends to be accurate. Astute negotiators realize that valuable knowledge can be gleaned simply by listening to everything their counterparts say, even seemingly extraneous or throwaway comments—in the same way that interrogators look for statements from criminal suspects that include facts not known to the public.

Even if your counterpart is determined to withhold information, you can still encourage leakage. In a series of experiments, my collaborators and I found that people are much more likely to let slip information about their engagement in sensitive behaviors than they are to explicitly divulge it. In one study, we probed *New York Times* readers about matters such as lying about their income. We directly asked people in one group if they had ever engaged in specific activities. We took an indirect approach with the other group,

In the Hot Seat: Handling Tough Questions Honestly

Information exchange is integral to creating win-win deals, but it must be carefully managed. Disclose too much and your counterpart might take advantage of you; disclose too little and you miss opportunities to discover mutually beneficial trades. So what should you do when you're asked a question that, if answered truthfully, would put you at a bargaining disadvantage?

What Not to Do

Lie. You will be tempted to lie. Don't. Setting aside ethical, moral, and legal arguments, if you get caught, it can damage your reputation and your relationship with your counterpart and potentially put the entire deal in peril. Research shows that many positive interactions are required to restore trust after a single breach, and breaches entailing deception are among the most difficult to recover from.

Palter. Another common but misguided approach is what Todd Rogers and colleagues call "paltering," or using truthful statements to convey an inaccurate impression. The researchers give the example of former U.S. president Bill Clinton's answer to a question about whether he'd had a sexual relationship with Monica Lewinsky: "There is not a sexual relationship—that is accurate." Technically that statement was not a lie, because his involvement with Lewinsky was in the past. But research shows that people view such legalistic skirting of the truth as unfavorably as they view outright lying.

asking participants to rate the ethicality of various behaviors using one of two scales—one scale if they themselves had engaged in the behavior and a different scale if they had not. Participants in the latter group were roughly 1.5 times likelier to admit (tacitly) to bad behavior than were people asked point-blank about their conduct.

In a negotiation, you might use similarly indirect tactics to glean information. For example, give your counterpart a choice of two different offer packages—two possible ways of dividing the spoils—both of which would be acceptable to you. If she expresses a preference for one over the other, she is leaking information about her

Abstain. A third common workaround is to abstain from answering the question. However, Kate Barasz, Michael Norton, and I have shown that this tactic leaves a worse impression than disclosing even extremely unsavory information. For example, in one study, participants viewed people who had confessed to frequently stealing items worth more than $100 as more trustworthy than those who had simply refused to answer the question.

What to Do

Redirect. In the short term, the strategies deployed by politicians, who routinely face tough, direct questions, can be instructive—particularly for one-shot negotiations (when you are unlikely to meet your counterpart again). A familiar tactic is to dodge the question by changing the subject to something seemingly related. As noted earlier, people are generally not very good at detecting dodges, so you have an opportunity to selectively disclose information of your choosing. A second strategy is to turn the tables and question the questioner. Responding in this way can deflect attention and enable you to take control of the topic.

Share carefully. If you're playing a longer game, disclosure can work in your favor; it can foster trust and facilitate better outcomes through collaboration and joint problem solving. To avoid being exploited, however, negotiators should start small: Share a substantive but not critical piece of information. Only if your counterpart reciprocates should you continue the tit for tat; disclosure without reciprocation leaves you vulnerable to your counterpart's value-claiming tactics.

priorities and giving you insight into her relative valuation of the issues up for negotiation.

Here's one more strategy that might encourage your counterpart to inadvertently show her hand: Request contingency clauses that attach financial consequences to her claims. If she balks at agreeing to them, it may be because she's lying. At a minimum, such a reaction should prompt you to probe further. Suppose, for example, that your business is negotiating the acquisition of a small start-up. Your counterpart gives you sales projections that strike you as optimistic or even impossible. You could propose a contingency clause that would tie the acquisition price to the sales level achieved. That would motivate your counterpart to provide realistic sales projections, and it would protect you if she's wrong.

———————————

Lying surrounds us—and can be a real impediment to the creation of value in negotiation. The good news is that deploying science-backed strategies can go a long way toward bringing out the best in negotiations—and in the parties involved.

Originally published in July–August 2016. Reprint R1607J

The Enemies
of Trust

by Robert M. Galford and Anne Seibold Drapeau

TRY AN EXPERIMENT SOMETIME. Ask a group of managers in your company whether they and their closest managerial colleagues are trustworthy and, if so, how they know. Most will claim that they themselves are trustworthy and that most of their colleagues are as well. Their answers to the second half of the question will likely reflect their beliefs about personal integrity; you'll hear things like "I'm straight with my people" or "She keeps her promises." A little later, ask them whether they think they and their colleagues are capable of building trust within the organization. Because we've asked this question many times, we're pretty sure we know what you'll hear: A sizable percentage will say they have little or no confidence in the group's capacity to build and maintain trust.

What accounts for the gap between the two sets of answers? With their differing responses, the managers are simply acknowledging a fact of organizational life: It takes more than personal integrity to build a trusting, trustworthy organization. It takes skills, smart supporting processes, and unwavering attention on the part of top managers. Trust within an organization is far more complicated and fragile than trust between, say, a consultant and a client. With a client, you can largely control the flow of communication. In an organization, people are bombarded with multiple, often contradictory messages every day. With a client, you can agree on desired outcomes up front. In an organization, different groups have different and often conflicting goals. With a client, you know if there's a problem. In an organization, there's a good chance you don't, even if you're in charge. If things aren't working out with a client, either party can walk away. That's not usually an option for people in an organization, so they stick around. But if they think the organization acted in bad faith, they'll rarely forgive—and they'll never forget.

Trust within an organization is further complicated by the fact that people use the word "trust" to refer to three different kinds. The first is *strategic trust*—the trust employees have in the people running the show to make the right strategic decisions. Do top managers have the vision and competence to set the right course, allocate resources intelligently, fulfill the mission, and help the company succeed? The second is *personal trust*—the trust employees have in their own managers. Do the managers treat employees fairly? Do they consider employees' needs when making decisions about the business and put the company's needs ahead of their own desires? The third is *organizational trust*—the trust people have not in any individual but in the company itself. Are processes well designed, consistent, and fair? Does the company make good on its promises? Clearly these three types of trust are distinct, but they're linked in important ways. Every time an individual manager violates the personal trust of her direct reports, for example, their organizational trust will be shaken.

As difficult as it is to build and maintain trust within organizations, it's critical. An established body of research demonstrates the links between trust and corporate performance. If people trust each other and their leaders, they'll be able to work through disagreements. They'll take smarter risks. They'll work harder, stay with the company longer, contribute better ideas, and dig deeper than anyone has a right to ask. If they don't trust the organization and its leaders, though, they'll disengage from their work and focus instead on rumors, politics, and updating their résumés. We know this because we've seen it happen many times and because a high percentage of consulting engagements that seem to be about strategic direction or productivity turn out to be about trust, or the lack thereof.

Idea in Brief

What is essential for top-notch corporate performance? Trust. It enables employees to resolve disagreements, take smarter risks, stay with the company longer, contribute better ideas, and dig deeper than anyone has a right to ask. Without it, people disengage from their work, focusing on rumors, politics, and résumé updating.

But trust is a complex, fragile thing—easier to destroy than to build and maintain. Its components are unsurprising: old-fashioned managerial virtues like consistency, clear communication, and a willingness to tackle awkward questions. Yet its enemies are legion.

Here's how to protect trust from its enemies and rebuild when it's damaged.

The building blocks of trust are unsurprising: They're old-fashioned managerial virtues like consistency, clear communication, and a willingness to tackle awkward questions. In our experience, building a trustworthy (and trusting) organization requires close attention to those virtues. But it also requires a defensive game: You need to protect trustworthiness from its enemies, both big and small, because trust takes years to build but can suffer serious damage in just a moment. We'll take a look at some of those enemies, discuss trust in times of crisis, and explore the ways to rebuild trust when it's been breached.

The Enemies List

What do the enemies of trust look like? Sometimes the enemy is a person: a first-line supervisor who habitually expresses contempt for top management. Sometimes it's knit into the fabric of the organization: a culture that punishes dissent or buries conflict. Some enemies are overt: You promise that this will be the last layoff, and then it isn't. And some are covert: A conversation you thought was private is repeated and then grossly distorted by the rumor mill. Because any act of bad management erodes trust, the list of enemies could be endless. Practically speaking, though, most breakdowns in trust that we've witnessed can be traced back to one of the following problems.

Inconsistent messages

One of the fastest-moving destroyers of trust, inconsistent messages can occur anywhere in an organization, from senior managers on down. They can also occur externally, in the way an organization communicates with its customers or other stakeholders. Either way, the repercussions are significant.

Consider the manager who tells employees in May that he's going to hold weekly brown-bag lunch meetings to discuss relevant issues in the marketplace. He implies that enthusiastic participation will be reflected in employees' performance reviews. But he then cancels the lunch the second, fourth, and fifth weeks because of his travel schedule. In week seven, he drops the idea entirely because, as he says, "With the summer here, we really can't count on a good turn-out." When he reintroduces the idea in October and insists it will work this time, do you think his employees believe him? And when it's time for performance reviews, do you think they are confident and trusting? No. They are confused and skeptical.

Senior executives often communicate inconsistent messages and priorities to various parts of the organization. We recently worked with a major financial institution in which top executives had repeatedly told members of the marketing staff that they were full business partners of the line organizations. Most of the executives in the line organizations, however, never heard that message and continued to treat marketing employees like low-level vendors. Why didn't top management communicate a consistent message? The answer is probably some combination of what we've seen in other companies: Senior managers tell people what they want to hear. And, all too often, senior managers across business units have widely disparate worldviews, which they communicate to their constituencies.

The antidotes to inconsistent messaging are straightforward (though they are not easy to implement): Think through your pri-orities. Before you broadcast them, articulate them to yourself or a trusted adviser to ensure that they're coherent and that you're being honest with people instead of making unrealistic commitments. Make sure your managerial team communicates a consistent message. Reserve big-bang announcements for truly major initiatives.

Inconsistent standards

If employees believe that an individual manager or the company plays favorites, their trust will be eroded. Employees keep score— relentlessly. Suppose that a company's offices in one city are palatial, and in another city employees make do with cramped cubicles. Local real estate prices most likely drive local decisions, but the people who end up with the warrens feel slighted nonetheless. Or suppose that the CEO took the new vice president of marketing out to lunch when he was promoted two months ago but failed to do the same when a new head of IT was appointed last week. There might be legitimate reasons for the CEO's inconsistent behavior, but the IT executive and the people around her will jump to the least-flattering, least-legitimate conclusion. Finally, suppose that the company's star performer is allowed to bend the rules while everyone else is expected to toe the line. As an executive, you may think it's worthwhile to let the most talented employee live by different rules in order to keep him. The problem is that your calculation doesn't take into account the cynicism you engender in the rest of the organization.

Misplaced benevolence

Managers know they have to do something about the employee who regularly steals, cheats, or humiliates coworkers. But most problematic behavior is subtler than that, and most managers have a hard time addressing it.

Consider incompetence. Anyone who has spent time in business has encountered at least one person who is, simply and sadly, so out of his league that everyone is stupefied that he's in the position at all. His colleagues wonder why his supervisors don't do something. His direct reports learn to work around him, but it's a daily struggle. Because the person in question isn't harming anyone or anything on purpose, his supervisor is reluctant to punish him. But incompetence destroys value, and it destroys all three kinds of trust.

Then there are the people with a cloud of negativity around them. These are often people who have been passed over for promotion or who feel they've been shortchanged on bonuses or salaries. They don't do anything outright to sabotage the organization, but they see the downside of everything. Their behavior often escapes management's attention, but their coworkers notice. After a while, people tire of their negative colleagues and may even catch the negativity bug themselves.

And, finally, people who are volatile—or just plain mean—often get away with appalling behavior because of their technical competence. Extremely ambitious people, similarly, tend to steamroll their colleagues, destroy teamwork, and put their own agendas ahead of the organization's interests. In both cases, ask yourself, "Is this person so valuable to the company that we should tolerate his behavior?"

Sometimes problematic employees can be transferred to more suitable jobs; sometimes they can be coached, trained, or surrounded by people who will help them improve; and sometimes they must be let go. The point is that they can't be ignored. Every time you let troubling behavior slide, everyone else feels the effects—and blames you.

False feedback
When an incompetent or otherwise unsuitable person is let go, managers often face wrongful-termination suits. "Look at these performance reviews," the supposed victim says. "They're great." And she is right: The performance reviews are great. The problem is that they're lies.

Being honest about employees' shortcomings is difficult, particularly when you have to talk to them about their performance regularly and face-to-face. But you must do it. If you don't honor your company's systems, you won't be able to terminate employees whose work is unacceptable. What's more, employees who are worthy of honest praise will become demoralized. "Why should I work this hard?" they will ask themselves. "So-and-so doesn't and everyone knows it, but I happen to know we got the same bonus."

You won't hear the complaint directly, but you'll see it in the lower quality of the competent employees' work.

Failure to trust others

Trusting others can be difficult, especially for a perfectionist or a workaholic. One top manager we worked with swore that he was going to delegate several important responsibilities. He brought in a new person at a senior level, but he was simply unable to trust her to do the work. After a few weeks, he began managing around her, issuing directives about things he had supposedly delegated and generally making her life miserable. Eventually, the manager's hoarding behavior left him isolated and hobbled. Just as important, the new employee didn't get a chance to develop professionally. Part of the implicit promise managers make is that employees will have a chance to grow. When managers don't give them that chance, the organization loses the trust of those employees, and the more talented among them leave.

Elephants in the parlor

Some situations are so painful or politically charged that it's easier to pretend they don't exist. We're talking about when someone has been fired abruptly and no one mentions it the next day at the regular staff meeting. We're talking about when an outrageous rumor finds its way to the CEO's office yet no one ever discusses it openly, even in private senior-management meetings.

Don't ignore things that you know everyone is whispering about behind closed doors. Bring such issues out into the open, explain them briefly, and answer questions as best you can. Don't be afraid to say, "I'm sorry, I can't offer more detail because that would violate a confidence." People will, sometimes grudgingly, accept the fact that they're not privy to all the gory details. But their trust in you will decline if they suspect you're trying to conceal something.

Rumors in a vacuum

When a company is in the throes of a complex initiative—a new product launch, say, or the analysis of a product line that has been underperforming—there are ample opportunities for trust to break down. Employees know that something important is going on, but if they don't know the full story (maybe the full story doesn't exist yet), they'll quite naturally overinterpret any shard of information they get their hands on. Rumors circulate, and, in most cases, they'll be negative rather than positive. Temporary information vacuums in corporate life are common, and distrust thrives in a vacuum.

What can you do? Be as up-front as possible—even if that means telling employees you can't say for certain what's going to happen. And be aware that the less you say, the more likely you are to be misinterpreted.

Michael Rice, head of Prudential Securities' Private Client Group, told us of a meeting during which a group of managers proposed some structural shifts that would affect the business's operations. In response to the presentation, Rice said, "The way you've described this, you're scaring me." The room fell silent, and the meeting ended awkwardly. One of his lieutenants explained that shortly after the last time Rice had said he was scared, there had been a large layoff. People picked up on the phrase and, since Rice hadn't described his objections more fully, they overinterpreted the comment.

You don't have to be a chatterbox to counter this enemy of trust, but do try to put yourself in your listeners' shoes. What don't they know about the situation at hand, and how will that affect what they hear? Are you saying enough? Or are you speaking in shorthand, either because you feel you can't share more information or because you assume people will understand what you're getting at?

Consistent corporate underperformance
If a company regularly fails to meet the expectations set by its senior management team (and adopted by Wall Street), trust erodes rapidly. Look at Kodak, Polaroid, and Xerox in times of decline. When an organization's performance is weaker than expected, a growing number of employees at all levels fear for themselves on a daily basis. They spend less and less time thinking for the organization and more and more time planning their own next moves. What can you do? Be realistic when setting expectations and communicate as much as

possible to all employees about why you're setting these goals and how the company can meet them. The more knowledge people have about what lies behind expectations, the more likely they are to continue trusting you and the company, even in tough times.

Trust in Tumultuous Times

As vigilant as you may be about fighting the enemies of trust that pop up in the course of doing business, there will be times when trust inside the organization is stressed to the maximum.

Perhaps the organization is undergoing a structural change like a merger, reorganization, or layoff (or all three). Under such circumstances, people's antennae are tuned to signals that might provide even a partial answer to the question, What does this mean for me? Memos and emails from senior managers, snatches of remembered conversations, phrases overheard in the parking lot—all of these are reread, rehashed, and analyzed word by word.

Don't be surprised when the things you say—including the most innocuous statements—are assigned deep, sinister meaning. People are also going to hold you accountable for what they *think* you said (which may not be what you think you said) for longer than you might believe. Consider all the organizations that announced they were "not currently planning any layoffs" but ultimately needed to reduce the workforce. When the layoff is announced, employees suspect that it was in the works when the first statement was issued, and they remind senior managers about the "promise." From the senior managers' point of view, no promise was made. Technically, that's true, but that truth isn't worth much. If you want to reassure people, don't speculate about the future. Instead, treat employees like grown-ups. In the case of a layoff, share the performance data or competitive situation that makes reductions necessary. And be extremely cautious about making unequivocal statements such as the following:

- I have no hidden agenda.

- There won't be any more layoffs.

- This time we've got it fixed.

- We will be stronger as a result.

- I have total faith in the senior management team.

- This is the hardest thing I've ever had to do.

Pronouncements like these can come back to haunt you. And they probably will.

Organizations also risk losing the trust of their people in times of crisis. Whether it is an episode of violence, an accident, or a serious product flaw, a corporate crisis can have a profound effect on a company's health. Often the damage occurs not because of the incident itself but because of how it's handled internally. Company leaders, or crisis team members, become so distracted by external pressures that they don't address the crisis internally with care and attention. That's dangerous, because employees feel unsafe during a crisis. They look for reasons to trust their leaders, but they are quick to find reasons why they *can't* trust them.

Mark Braverman, a senior vice president with Marsh Crisis Consulting in Washington, DC, says companies that respond well to customers during crises very often neglect their own employees. Recovering revenues is important, as is moving the company out of the media spotlight. But calls from reporters, shareholders, and customers shouldn't be given so much attention that you ignore what's going on with the people who show up every day to work. You want things to go back to normal, so your tendency is to deal first with the people you don't "normally" have to deal with. But your people will not be able to wait until the flurry subsides. By the time you turn to them, the damage may be beyond repair.

Under extreme stress, normally competent managers may feel fragile, guilty, overwhelmed, and unable to cope. It's hard to act like a leader when you're experiencing those emotions. But employees feel just as much stress as you do, and they need calm, visible leadership far more than they normally do. If you "go dark" in the face of a crisis, employees worry about how the company will survive, about whether you're up to the task, and about their own capacity

Uncomfortable Truths About Organizational Life

There's no such thing as a private conversation. We don't say this to make you paranoid, and maybe you have a confidant who's truly discreet. But in general you should assume that everything you say will circulate to the people who would be most affected by it.

There's no such thing as a casual conversation. People will attempt to read deep meaning into your most innocuous comments and movements.

People sometimes hear what they most fear. In some organizations, under some circumstances, people will immediately jump to the most paranoid, negative interpretation of *all* your comments and movements.

Trauma has a long half-life. You will likely find yourself apologizing for misdeeds that you did not commit and for events that occurred before you arrived.

No good deed goes unpunished. Even if you act with the purest intentions and execute with the greatest skill, someone will object to your actions or to the results you achieve.

Newton's third law doesn't always apply. Newton said that every action has an equal and opposite reaction, but you may take a small, seemingly harmless step that has a huge, negative impact. Or you may make what you think is a dramatic, deeply meaningful change, only to hear people say, "Okay, good. Now, what's for lunch?"

---

to cope. When everyone worries, trust evaporates. The first lesson here is to get yourself some help. If you were not directly affected by the crisis, you may need only a quick check-in with an objective third party. But if you were directly affected, don't assume that you are thinking clearly. Your perspective may be off. Acknowledging that fact could save you from some painful mistakes and could save employees and other stakeholders a lot of pain as well.

The second lesson is not to withdraw. Let it be known that you're aware of the situation and that you'll keep everyone posted as events unfold and as decisions are made. Set an update schedule and keep to it, even if the update is that there will be no news until next week. Just as important, be physically and emotionally accessible to the people around you. They want to know that it is okay to have feelings at work about whatever is going on. They'll look to you to set the example. And that means you have to allow yourself to do some of the things that you may have thought being a leader meant you *couldn't* do. If you're shaken, for example, say so, even as you strive to provide stable ground from which to move the organization forward. If you feel like stopping work for a few hours, or even a day, just to talk about what happened in an informal way, do it. Let people know that you are taking the time to think through what has happened, and that it is fine for them to follow suit.

Starting Over

There are times when, inevitably, trust will be badly damaged somewhere in your organization, and there's nothing you can do to stop the breakdown. Your only choice, other than finding a different job, is to rebuild. We recommend that you follow these four steps.

First, figure out what happened. That may sound simple, but it rarely is. To build your own understanding, consider these questions.

- How quickly or slowly did trust break down? If it happened fast, don't expect rapid remediation. Most of us aren't as good at forgiving as we'd like to be. If trust was lost over a period of time, it's helpful to think about the deterioration process in order to identify how to prevent such failures in the future.

- When did the violation of trust become known to you and to the larger organization? If you've known that something was amiss but failed to acknowledge the loss of trust or respond appropriately for a considerable period of time, that lag will compound employees' feelings of betrayal.

- Was there a single cause? It's easier to address a onetime event than a pattern of events, but don't be too quick to assume the problem is simple. Remember: Every organization has a few conspiracy theorists, and the perception of a conspiracy can damage trust as devastatingly as a real one can.

- Was the loss of trust reciprocal? If your trust was violated and others say that theirs was, too, chances are no one will behave fairly or objectively. It's acceptable to be angry when your trust has been betrayed. But retaliatory or vindictive? Never. We've seen organizations spiral downward as people try to hurt others who have violated their trust. If you discern that the loss of trust in your organization is reciprocal and deep-seated, a formal process of conflict resolution might be in order.

Second, when you have a reasonably good handle on what happened, ascertain the depth and breadth of the loss of trust. A sense of how much of the organization has been affected will help you avoid situations in which you try to put out a lit match with a full muster of fire-fighters or, by contrast, an inferno with spit. Imagine the challenges facing the management committee of a *Fortune* 500 investment bank after a stockbroker in a Midwestern branch was discovered to have defrauded clients out of many millions. The impact on the branch's other clients was severe, and the impact on clients elsewhere in the Midwest was also substantial. However, the reaction on the West Coast was highly varied: Many clients weren't even aware of the breach. A different level of response was required for different groups of clients.

Third, own up to the loss quickly instead of ignoring or downplaying it. Employees will be skeptical or suspicious, or both, so you'll need to choose your words carefully. But acknowledging that trust has been damaged and starting the recovery process as quickly as possible can only be to your benefit. You don't have to have all the answers or a detailed plan. There can even be a lag between naming the problem and describing what you'll do. Just let people know that you're aware of the issue and its impact on them and that you're committed to setting things right. Let them know when they will hear more from you, and stick to that time frame, even if all you can say at that point is that you're not yet ready to say anything.

Fourth, identify as precisely as possible what you must accomplish in order to rebuild trust. For example, you might need to change the relationship between people in the sales offices and people at headquarters from an adversarial one to a cooperative one. Or you might want to have people stop doing end runs around a department that has a reputation for arrogance. Then give yourself examples of what success will look like in practice. For example, "The quarterly review meetings will spend 50% less time on mediating disputes and 50% more time on planning new initiatives." Or "We will establish clear roles and responsibilities, an exceptions policy, a dispute resolution process, and submission and response protocols."

Then list the changes you'll make in organizational structure, systems, people, and culture to achieve those outcomes. What specific shifts (if any) will you make in how decisions are made, how information flows, and how it is measured, reported, compensated for, and rewarded? Should some reporting relationships be changed? Which areas might be merged, consolidated, or separated? We have seen internal rivalries dissolve almost instantaneously when competing areas come under the control of a single person. And we've been amazed at how quickly trust (and productivity) improves when the move is finally made to replace a key player who has done a poor job of building trust inside a group.

Keep an eye on practical issues: How will these valuable changes and initiatives happen? How much of the work will you do yourself, what will you delegate, and how much will be done in teams? What's a reasonable time frame for getting things done? (Some efforts will probably be ongoing, while others will be more finite.) And keep an eye on the trust recovery mission in its entirety. Very often, such missions suffer from an imbalance of short-term measures at the expense of longer-term efforts. They are also frequently tilted too much in favor of those directly affected at the expense of the broader organization. Looking hard at the plan (and asking one or two people who were not a part of its creation to scrutinize it as well) can save a great deal of time and resources down the road.

Trust within organizations isn't easy to pin down. It's hard to measure, even in a quick-and-dirty way. And suppose you could measure it perfectly—the truth is that no company would ever get a perfect score. Organizations and people are too complicated for that. Nor is it easy to define the trustworthy leader. Some exude emotional intelligence; others appear to be rather boring, extremely consistent bureaucrats. And, being human, even the best of them occasionally make mistakes that erode trust. But trust is the crucial ingredient of organizational effectiveness. Building it, maintaining it, and restoring it when it is damaged must be at the top of every chief executive's agenda.

Originally published in February 2003. Reprint R0302G

Don't Let Cynicism Undermine Your Workplace

by Jamil Zaki

AN OPEN CEO ROLE AT MICROSOFT should be the holy grail for executives in the tech industry, but that wasn't the case in 2014. The company's growth had stagnated. By botching early leads on smartphones and other new technologies, Microsoft had lost market share to Apple, Google, and Amazon and had gained a reputation as creaky and out of touch—a giant ship lurching in the wrong direction.

The Bloomberg journalist Dina Bass listed those downsides in an article bluntly titled "Why You Don't Want to Be Microsoft CEO." Five days later Satya Nadella took the helm. Microsoft's failures stemmed from a deeper problem: a culture mired in mistrust, competition, and tribalism, which killed morale and stifled innovation. In his 2017 book, *Hit Refresh,* Nadella described an illustration of Microsoft's org chart by the designer Manu Cornet that showed the company's divisions in a standoff, with circles representing rigid silos aiming guns at one another. The cartoon was meant to be funny, but the problems it highlighted weren't. Nor are they rare.

Countless organizations have been overrun by cynicism—a belief that other people are selfish, greedy, and dishonest. Texas A&M's Dan Chiaburu and his coauthors have found that cynicism predicts a slew of negative outcomes at work, including poor performance, burnout, turnover, and cheating. Cynicism also spreads rapidly.

People with a dim view of others' actions gossip and are prone to backstabbing—behavior that brings out the worst in their colleagues, causing the cynics' suspicion and mistrust to become self-fulfilling prophecies.

Fortunately you can take steps to avoid that scenario. Decades' worth of research—my own and others'—offers insight into how people fall into the *cynicism trap,* how an organization's policies and practices may be responsible, and what leaders can do to help employees escape it.

The Cynicism Trap

When we look at the world through a cynical lens, people appear to be out for themselves, acts of kindness hide ulterior motives, and trusting others makes you a sucker. That way of thinking is understandable in the age of WeWork and Theranos. But too much cynicism can become toxic at every level. Individually, cynics earn less money over the course of their lives, are more likely to experience depression, and are at greater risk of heart disease than noncynics are. And Microsoft is just one example of how detrimental cynicism can be to organizations and work life.

Despite its dire consequences, cynicism appears to be on the rise. In 1972, 45% of Americans believed that "most people can be trusted," according to the General Social Survey. By 2018 that share had dropped to about 30%. In the 2022 edition of the annual Edelman Trust Barometer, nearly 60% of people across 27 countries said their default is to distrust others. And people aren't skeptical of individuals only: Over the same period trust in political leaders, institutions, and corporations plummeted as well.

Why is cynicism so widespread, even though it hurts us so much? Some reasons are cultural. In countries and states with rampant corruption and inequality, cynicism takes hold more quickly. Professions have cultural inducements as well: Journalists succeed by sniffing out lies, and start-up founders are often incentivized to exaggerate—which significantly contributes to mistrust.

Idea in Brief

The Problem

Too many organizations are marked by cynicism—a belief that others are selfish, greedy, and dishonest—which predicts a slew of negative outcomes at work, including poor performance, turnover, cheating, and stifled innovation.

Why It Happens

Our natural pull toward negativity and the notion that cynics are smarter than noncynics allow

cynicism to self-perpetuate. Organizational policies and practices can further reinforce a culture of mistrust.

How to Fix It

You can reduce cynicism in your organization by developing policies and processes that redirect the organizational culture toward collaboration and by making sure that all leaders—not just those at the top—model trusting behaviors and combat cynicism in their interactions.

Cynicism also takes advantage of bugs in the way people think and feel. By understanding three of its drivers—*badness attunement, preemptive strikes,* and the *cynical-genius illusion*—you can take steps to eradicate it from your organization.

Badness attunement

The greatest threat to human beings is other people, who may cheat, steal, and take advantage of our trust. Nature's answer to such social threats is to equip us with a psychological armadillo shell—what scientists call "cheater detection." From an early age we are vigilant for signs that someone may be trying to pull one over on us. Cheater detection helps us distinguish between bad actors (such as crooks and swindlers) and good ones, but it can also cause us to assume that people are bad and to focus on their worst qualities. Psychologists call this "positive-negative asymmetry," but let's call it badness attunement.

A Russian proverb holds that "a drop of tar spoils a barrel of honey." Our social judgments can work the same way. In what's now considered a classic pair of studies, the researchers John Skowronski and Donal Carlston told people about someone who acted morally (helping strangers), immorally (cheating on taxes), or a combination of the two. People judged immoral actors more quickly than they praised moral ones and considered people who acted in both ways to be morally tainted.

In other words, we imagine a version of others that is much worse than the flesh-and-blood folks actually out there. And when we interact with that version rather than with their true selves, our responses can cause harm and spread cynicism further.

Preemptive strikes

Cynics often act as though the best defense is a good offense. In my lab's recent research we found that cynical individuals—those who disagree with statements such as "Most people are generally good"—are less willing to donate time or money to help others. Another study, led by Malia Mason at Columbia University, reveals that people who consider others dishonest are more likely to negotiate dishonestly themselves.

Preemptive strikes may look savvy, but they hurt everyone involved. People reciprocate kindness and retaliate against cruelty, meaning that cynics' actions bring out the worst in others. In a 2020 survey psychologists explored those self-fulfilling prophecies by asking people about their social interactions once a day for a week. They found that a cynic tends to act disrespectfully toward friends and colleagues, which increases others' disrespect for the cynic. And in one prominent study the psychologists Harold Kelley and Anthony Stahelski asked pairs of people to play a game in which they could either cooperate or cheat. Because cynics expected their partners to cheat, they were more likely to begin the game by cheating. In subsequent rounds cynics' partners were less likely to trust and more likely to cheat as well, which the researchers call "behavioral assimilation."

The cynical-genius illusion

Self-proclaimed cynics often view their cynicism as hard-earned wisdom and consider anyone who doesn't share it to be naive. In research led by Olga Stavrova of Tilburg University, 70% of participants said they believed that cynics are generally smarter than noncynics—even though the former don't perform as well on cognitive tests and are not "socially smart." In another study Nancy Carter and J. Mark Weber of the University of Toronto Mississauga conducted mock job interviews in which they asked half the candidates to lie and half to tell the truth. Participants watched videos of the interviews and guessed who was lying, and although 85% of participants believed that cynics are better equipped to detect liars, people who had self-identified as cynics were actually less accurate with their guesses.

Although they may accuse others of blindly trusting, it seems that cynics themselves blindly *mistrust*. By viewing everyone through the same dark lens, they fail to notice cues that distinguish cooperators from cheaters. Yet as long as people continue believing that cynicism is smart, cynics will be rewarded.

How Policies and Practices Breed Cynicism

It's not just human psychology that drives employees toward mistrust. It's quite possible that your company's policies and practices are based on and reinforce cynicism as well, as was the case at Microsoft. Nadella's predecessor, Steve Ballmer, made decisions and created policies that bred distrust and corrosive competition. Two of Ballmer's strategies—zero-sum leadership and overmanaging—are common in many organizations.

Zero-sum leadership

Ballmer implemented "stack ranking," whereby top performers on each team reaped rewards while stragglers were warned or fired. Stack ranking is meant to tap into people's "natural" competitiveness, but it also causes employees to see their workplace as a zero-sum game. In a 2012 *Vanity Fair* article Kurt Eichenwald laid out the policy's effects: "Staffers were rewarded not just for doing well but for making sure that their colleagues failed. As a result, the company was consumed by an endless series of internal knife fights. Potential market-busting businesses—such as e-book and smartphone technology—were killed, derailed, or delayed amid bickering and power plays."

Few organizations use stack ranking today, but many still promote a "culture of genius" that values the lone creative star who comes up with new ideas. Such a culture encourages people to outshine colleagues, sparking unhealthy competition. When workers are pitted against one another, they have little reason to contribute to collective ideas and are more likely to hide knowledge from their peers—damaging relationships and killing innovation. A research team led by Elizabeth Canning, a professor at Washington State University, found that *Fortune* 500 companies with cultures of genius have lower levels of employee trust and receive worse ratings on Glassdoor.

Overmanaging

In *The HP Way,* David Packard tells a story from his early career at GE, when the company locked up and closely monitored computer parts to prevent theft. "Faced with this obvious display of distrust," Packard writes, "employees set out to prove it justified, walking off with tools or parts whenever they could."

Leaders who don't trust their people are more likely to restrict, pressure, and surveil them to ensure that they do the bare minimum and to prevent shirking and cheating—and employees read that mistrust loud and clear. They in turn trust their organizations less, feel less motivated, and are—ironically—*more* likely to game the system.

The pandemic has made it harder to hover over people's desks, but companies now use a dystopian array of tools that enable them to, for instance, monitor workers' keystrokes and screens. In response, online retailers have sold thousands of "mouse jigglers," which allow users to appear to be working. (An Amazon review of one such product reads, "If your boss is a micromanaging worthless idiot who doesn't realize that presence does not equate to productivity, this is the device. If you are one of those bosses reading this review . . . nobody likes you.")

When employers force workers to do at least the bare minimum, they make it much more likely that workers will do *only* that—and morale is harmed in the process. In December 2021 EY released new data on employees who had left their jobs during the first part of the Great Resignation. Many of them said they didn't feel that company leaders cared about or trusted them.

Escaping the Cynicism Trap

This picture can be bleak: Mistrust and competition seem to be taking us on a one-way street toward failure. Fortunately, there are clear strategies that can help organizations reverse course. Injecting "anticynicism" into yours requires implementing two approaches: First, develop policies and processes that redirect the organizational culture toward collaboration and trust. Second, make sure that all leaders—not just those at the top—model trusting behaviors and combat cynicism in their interactions.

Redirect the culture

In his book Nadella commented on the cartoon Microsoft org chart: "The caricature really bothered me. But what upset me more was that our own people just accepted it." He and Microsoft's chief people officer, Kathleen Hogan, introduced policies meant to undo the company's cynical habits, including a restructuring of Microsoft's review and incentive system. No longer would employees be elevated for outshining their peers—or punished if their peers excelled. Instead they were reviewed and rewarded for collaborative behavior, such as how they showed up for others and created things together. That shift encouraged workers to lower their defenses and share knowledge, skills, and perspectives freely. Such "task interdependence," whereby individual success rests on the achievements of others, increases trust among employees and strengthens the chances of trust and team success.

Nadella took a similar approach to Microsoft's competitors. In a move that would have been unthinkable the year before, he walked onstage for an industry keynote and pulled out an iPhone equipped for the first time with Office, Outlook, and other Microsoft products. By showing how Microsoft and Apple could complement each other, Nadella not only de-escalated their rivalry but also provided a benefit to consumers. "Partnering is too often seen as a zero-sum game," he wrote in his book. Both inside and outside Microsoft, Nadella sought win-win solutions to grow the pie—tapping into people's collaborative instincts rather than their selfishness.

When we see the world as zero-sum, it shrinks, and so do our partnerships. Anticynicism may seem naive, but it turns out to be the wiser long-term strategy.

Model trust

Nadella encouraged employees to learn and take greater creative risks, such as in enormous hackathons—collaborative coding runs in which groups worked on a free-for-all of fresh ideas. Those ideas helped Microsoft move beyond software and into cloud and AI technology. Bringing them to fruition also required a loosening of the bureaucratic reins—and a leap of faith by the company's leadership.

People we put faith in are more likely to step up, demonstrating what economists call "earned trust." In one study Gerardo Guerra and Daniel John Zizzo asked people to play a game: Trusters sent money to trustees, and the money was multiplied. Trustees could choose how much to repay the truster from the larger amount of money. In another study Guerra, Zizzo, and Michael Bacharach asked trusters to guess in advance what trustees would do with the money. Trustees who were told about trusters' high expectations were more likely to pay them back.

If cynical beliefs can become self-fulfilling, hopeful ones can too, as this study and many others show.

Demonstrating faith in people is an easy way for leaders to reduce mistrust and paranoia in their organizations. Give people room to make their own choices. When you cultivate trust, teams excel. Research on teachers, retail workers, and army personnel finds that those who feel trusted experience greater self-esteem and connection to supervisors and ultimately perform better, too.

Nordstrom takes this idea seriously. The company's "employee handbook" is a single card, which reads in part: "Set your personal and professional goals high. We have great confidence in your ability to achieve them, so our employee handbook is very simple. We have only one rule. . . . Use good judgment in all situations."

Employees at Nordstrom are supported—they can turn to HR or managers at any time—but they are also explicitly trusted, which isn't the norm in the retail industry. The result is a famously satisfied workforce, which in 2017 made Nordstrom the only clothing retailer on *Fortune*'s list of the 100 best companies for employees. An important lesson is that when you trust people, do it loudly: Let them know you believe in them. They will be more likely to see themselves positively through your eyes and want to live up to that image.

At Microsoft anticynical practices such as creating non-zero-sum outcomes and giving workers space and trust to create have paid dividends. Under Nadella's stewardship the company's market capitalization skyrocketed because of its nimble moves into cloud computing, artificial intelligence, and other new frontiers—innovations nourished by a culture that centers on collaboration, empathy, and community.

Teach Anticynicism

Redirecting a company's culture and modeling trust can begin to untie the knots that cynicism creates. But you also need to change the way leaders at all levels interact with employees. The good news? Anticynicism can be taught.

In 2020 I teamed up with the SAP Academy for Engineering and Mentora to create a multidisciplinary leadership training program, which we have shared with more than 100 managers around the world. SAP's academy is renowned for teaching technical skills, but it had done less teaching of soft skills such as empathy and anticynicism. We challenged managers to think of those practices as just as important, and just as learnable, as any type of code.

One pillar of the program is building trust. Leaders learn about the perils of cynicism and pick up practical strategies for combating it. We show them that the best way to inspire trust in employees is to demonstrate it first. The results have been remarkable. Managers in our program saw their Net Promoter Score on leadership trust—a core index of how they are viewed by direct reports—increase by more than 10%.

That statistic encouraged us, as did the stories we heard from participating managers. One of them, Alejandra, had experienced a meteoric rise at SAP Brazil. In 14 months she went from being an individual contributor to leading a team of 22 people, many of whom had been with the company longer than she had. Her advancement created some resentment, and Alejandra felt the need to prove herself by tightly managing the group. She quickly became exhausted, as did her team.

After one anticynicism session, Alejandra met with a newer team member, an ambitious and talented individual who wanted more independence but feared failure. Before our session Alejandra would have watched this person closely, but this time she took a different tack. "I know you can do this," she said, "and if you trust me, then you should trust my judgment." Six months later that employee was applying for leadership roles herself.

Here is a key principle of this work—and of anticynicism in general: People are shaped by their situations, and as leaders, you are an essential part of the situation for your employees. If you mistrust, micromanage, and monitor them, they will resent you, shirk responsibility, and eventually head for the exit. But if you show faith in them, they will try to live up to it. People become who we think they are, so we should be conscious of our assumptions and generous with our goodwill. It can make a bigger difference than we may imagine.

Trust is only one component of anticynical leadership. Leaders should also examine structural factors in their workplace: Are your corporate values mere window dressing, or do you deliver on them in concrete ways? Are wages, bonuses, and benefits fairly and transparently determined? If those conditions are not met, no amount of kind conversation will defeat cynicism.

Microsoft and Nordstrom demonstrate the importance of corporate policies that center on collaboration and openness; Alejandra's story shows us how individual leaders can promote those ideas. Leaders who make use of both approaches are well equipped to combat the cynicism trap—and to reap the benefits for themselves, their employees, and their organizations.

Originally published in September–October 2022. Reprint R2205D

The Trust Crisis

by Sandra J. Sucher and Shalene Gupta

BUSINESSES PUT AN AWFUL LOT OF EFFORT into meeting the diverse needs of their stakeholders—customers, investors, employees, and society at large. But they're not paying enough attention to one ingredient that's crucial to productive relationships with those stakeholders: trust.

Trust, as defined by organizational scholars, is our willingness to be vulnerable to the actions of others because we believe they have good intentions and will behave well toward us. In other words, we let others have power over us because we think they won't hurt us and will in fact help us. When we decide to interact with a company, we believe it won't deceive us or abuse its relationship with us. However, trust is a double-edged sword. Our willingness to be vulnerable also means that our trust can be betrayed. And over and over, businesses have betrayed stakeholders' trust.

Consider Facebook. In April 2018, CEO Mark Zuckerberg came before Congress and was questioned about Facebook's commitment to data privacy after it came to light that the company had exposed the personal data of 87 million users to the political consultant Cambridge Analytica, which used it to target voters during the 2016 U.S. presidential election. Then, in September, Facebook admitted that hackers had gained access to the log-in information of 50 million of its users. The year closed out with a New York Times investigation revealing that Facebook had given Netflix, Spotify, Microsoft, Yahoo, and Amazon access to its users' personal data, including in some cases their private messages.

So, in the middle of last year, when Zuckerberg announced that Facebook would launch a dating app, observers shook their heads. And this past April, when the company announced it was releasing an app that allowed people to share photos and make video calls on its smart-home gadget Portal, TechCrunch observed that "critics were mostly surprised by the device's quality but too freaked out to recommend it." Why would we trust Facebook with personal data on something as sensitive as dating—or with a camera and microphone—given its horrible track record?

Volkswagen is still struggling with the aftermath of the 2015 revelation that it cheated on emissions tests. United Airlines has yet to fully recover from two self-inflicted wounds: getting security to drag a doctor off a plane after he resisted giving up his seat in 2017, and the death of a puppy on a plane in 2018 after a flight attendant insisted its owner put it in an overhead bin. In the spring of 2019 Boeing had to be forced by a presidential order to ground its 737 Max jets in the United States, even though crashes had killed everyone on board two planes in five months and some 42 other countries had forbidden the jets to fly. Later the news broke that Boeing had known there was a problem with the jet's safety features as early as 2017 but failed to disclose it. Now, customers, pilots and crew, and regulators all over the world are wondering why they should trust Boeing. Whose interests was it serving?

Betrayals of trust have major financial consequences. In 2018 the Economist studied eight of the largest recent business scandals, comparing the companies involved with their peer groups, and found that they had forfeited significant amounts of value. The median firm was worth 30% less than it would have been valued had it not experienced a scandal. That same year another study, by IBM Security and Ponemon Institute, put the average cost of a data breach at $3.86 million, a 6.4% increase over the year before, and calculated that on average each stolen record cost a company $148.

Creating trust, in contrast, lifts performance. In a 1999 study of Holiday Inns, 6,500 employees rated their trust in their managers on a scale of 1 to 5. The researchers found that a one-eighth point improvement in scores could be expected to increase an inn's annual profits by 2.5% of revenues, or $250,000 more per hotel. No other aspect of managers' behavior had such a large impact on profits.

Trust also has macro-level benefits. A 1997 study of 29 market economies across one decade by World Bank economists showed that a 10-percentage-point increase in trust in an environment was correlated with a 0.8-percentage-point bump in per capita income growth.

So our need to trust and be trusted has a very real economic impact. More than that, it deeply affects the fabric of society. If we can't trust other people, we'll avoid interacting with them, which will make it hard to build anything, solve problems, or innovate.

Building trust isn't glamorous or easy. And at times it involves making complex decisions and difficult trade-offs.

In her 15 years of research into what trusted companies do, Sandra has found—no surprise—that they have strong relationships with all their main stakeholders. But the behaviors and processes that built those relationships *were* surprising. She has distilled her findings into a framework that can help companies nurture and maintain trust. It explains the basic promises stakeholders expect a company to keep, the four ways they evaluate companies for trustworthiness, and five myths that prevent companies from rebuilding trust.

What Stakeholders Want

Companies can't build trust unless they understand the fundamental promises they make to stakeholders. Firms have three kinds of responsibilities: *Economically,* people count on them to provide value. *Legally,* people expect them to follow not just the letter of the law but also its spirit. *Ethically,* people want companies to pursue moral ends, through moral means, for moral motives.

What this looks like varies with each kind of stakeholder. To customers, for instance, economic value means creating products and services that enhance their lives; to employees, it means a livelihood; to investors, it means returns; and to society, it means both fulfilling important needs and providing growth and prosperity. Here's the complete set of stakeholder expectations:

The fundamental promises of business

Stakeholder	Economic promise	Legal promise	Ethical promise
Customers	• To provide products and services that enhance their lives	• To follow consumer protection laws and industry regulations	• To make good on commitments • To disclose risks • To remediate mistakes made or harm done
Employees	• To provide a livelihood (pay, benefits, training, opportunity)	• To follow labor, antidiscrimination, and workplace safety laws	• To provide safe work conditions and job security • To treat everyone fairly
Investors	• To provide returns • To manage risk	• To fulfill fiduciary duties • To disclose material information	• To oversee employees' conduct • To abstain from insider trading and self-dealing
Society	• To offer employment and economic development • To fulfill important needs	• To follow local and federal laws • To work with regulators	• To protect public health, the environment, and the local community • To set industry standards

Of course, expectations can vary within a stakeholder group, leading to ambiguity about what companies need to live up to. Investors are a prime example. Some believe the only duty of a company is to maximize shareholder returns, while others think companies have an obligation to create positive societal effects by employing sound environmental, social, and governance practices.

How Stakeholders Evaluate Trust

Trust is multifaceted: Not only do stakeholders depend on businesses for different things, but they may trust an organization in some ways but not others. To judge the worthiness of companies, stakeholders continually ask four questions. Let's look at each in turn.

Is the company competent?

At the most fundamental level companies are evaluated on their ability to create and deliver a product or service. There are two aspects to this:

Technical competence refers to the nuts and bolts of developing, manufacturing, and selling products or services. It includes the ability to innovate, to harness technological advances, and to marshal resources and talent.

Social competence involves understanding the business environment and sensing and responding to changes. A company must have insight into different markets and what offerings may be attractive to them now and in the future. It also needs to recognize how competition is shifting and know how to work with partners such as suppliers, government authorities, regulators, NGOs, the media, and unions.

In the short term technical competence wins customers, but in the long run social competence is necessary to build a company that can navigate a constantly evolving business landscape.

Consider Uber. The company has weathered an avalanche of scandals, including reports of sexual harassment, a toxic corporate culture, and shady business practices in 2017, which led to CEO Travis Kalanick's departure. Uber's losses that year came to $4.5 billion. And yet, by the end of 2018, Uber was operating in 63 countries and had 91 million active monthly users. We love Uber, we hate Uber, and sometimes we leave Uber. We keep using Uber not because we don't care about its mistakes but because Uber fills a need and does it well. Consumers trust that when they put an order into Uber a car will arrive to pick them up. We forget how difficult that is to do. In 2007, two years before Uber's launch, an app called Taxi Magic entered the market. Taxi Magic worked with fleet owners, and drivers leased cars from the fleet owners, so there was little accountability. If a cab saw another passenger on its way to pick up a Taxi Magic rider, it might abandon the Taxi Magic customer. In 2009, another start-up, Cabulous, also created an app that people could use to book rides. However, that app often didn't work, and Cabulous had no means of regulating supply and demand, so taxi drivers wouldn't turn on the app when they were busy. Neither business achieved anything on the scale of Uber. We might have mixed feelings about Uber's surge pricing, but it helps make sure there are enough drivers on the road to meet demand.

Meanwhile, on a social level Uber has managed to transform the taxi industry. Before Uber, cities limited the number of taxis in the streets by requiring drivers to purchase medallions. In 2013, a medallion in New York City could cost as much as $1.32 million. Such sky-high prices made it difficult for newcomers to enter the market, and lack of competition meant drivers had little incentive to provide good service. Uber brought new drivers into the market, improved service, and increased accessibility to rides in areas with limited taxi coverage.

Still, we use Uber with mixed feelings. Uber achieved much of its growth by quickly acquiring capital, which allowed it to develop technology for fast pickups and to offer drivers high pay and riders low fares. At the same time it was a ruthless competitor that reportedly was not above using underhanded tactics, such as ordering and then cancelling Lyft rides (a charge Uber denied) and misleading drivers about their potential earnings.

We don't trust Uber to treat its employees or customers well or to conduct business cleanly. In other words we don't trust Uber's motives, means, or impact. This has consequences. Although Uber was projected to reach 44 million users in 2017, it hit only 41 million. Since then Uber's growth has continued to be lower than expected, and the company has ceded market share to Lyft. This year Uber's much-anticipated IPO underperformed after thousands of Uber drivers went on strike to protest their working conditions. The company's stock price fell by 11% after its first earnings report for 2019 revealed that it had lost more than $1 billion in its first quarter.

Is the company motivated to serve others' interests as well as its own?

Stakeholders need to believe a company is doing what's good for them, not just what's best for itself. However, stakeholders' concerns and goals aren't all the same. While many actions can serve multiple parties, companies must figure out how to prioritize stakeholder interests and avoid harming one group in an attempt to benefit another.

To determine whether they're doing right by all of their stakeholders, companies should examine their own motivations—by asking these three questions:

- Do we tell the truth?

- On whose behalf are we acting?

- Do our actions actually benefit those who trust us?

Honeywell is an example of a company that works hard to serve—and balance—the needs of all its stakeholders. Let's look at what happened there during the Great Recession, when it needed to reduce costs but wanted to keep making good on stakeholder expectations. Dave Cote, Honeywell's CEO at the time, explained how the company thought about that challenge: "We have these three constituencies we have to manage. If we don't do a great job with customers, both employees and investors will get hurt. So we said our first priority is customers. We need to make sure we can still deliver, that it's a quality product, and that if we've committed to a project, it will get done on time."

For investors and employees, he continued, "we have to balance the pain, because if you're in the middle of a recession, there's going to be pain . . . . Investors need to know they can count on the company, that we're also going to be doing all the right things for the long term, but we're thinking about them. After all, they're the owners of the company, and we work for them. . . . But at the same time we need to recognize that the employees are the base for success in the future . . . and we need to be thoughtful about how we treat them. And I think if you get the balance right between those two, yeah, investors might not be as happy in the short term if you could have generated more earnings, but they're definitely going to be happier in the longer term. Employees might not be as happy in the short term because they might have preferred that you just say to heck with all the investors. But in the long term they're going to benefit also because you're going to have a much more robust company for them to be part of."

During the recession, Honeywell used furloughs, rather than lay-offs, to lower payroll costs. But it limited the scale and duration of the furloughs by first implementing a hiring freeze, eliminating wage increases, reducing overtime, temporarily halting the employee rewards and recognition program, and cutting the company match for 401(k)s from 100% to 50%. The company distributed a reduced bonus pool as restricted stock so that employees could share in the stock's post-recovery upside. And Cote and his entire leadership team refused to take a bonus in 2009, reinforcing the message of shared pain.

To protect customers' interests during the downturn, Honeywell came up with the idea of placing advance orders with suppliers that the company would activate as soon as sales picked up. Suppliers were happy with the guaranteed production, and Honeywell stole a march on its competitors by filling customer orders faster than they could as the recovery began.

In the long run, those moves paid off for investors. During the recovery, from 2009 to 2012, they were rewarded with a 75% increase in Honeywell's total stock value—which was 20 percentage points higher than the stock value increase of its nearest competitor.

Cote also built trust with the public by moving from a previous approach of litigating claims for asbestos and environmental damage to settling them. Honeywell began to issue payouts of $150 million for claims annually, making its liabilities more manageable and easing investors' worries about future litigation costs. Cote also systematically went about cleaning up contaminated sites. That kind of attention to the interests of stakeholders gave people faith in the company's good intentions.

Does the company use fair means to achieve its goals?

A company's approach to dealing with customers, employees, investors, and society often comes under scrutiny. Companies that are trusted are given more leeway to create rules of engagement. Companies that aren't face regulation. Just ask Facebook.

To build strong trust, firms need to understand—and measure up on—four types of fairness that organizational scholars have identified:

- *Procedural fairness:* Whether good processes, based on accurate data, are used to make decisions and are applied consistently, and whether groups are given a voice in decisions affecting them

- *Distributive fairness:* How resources (such as pay and promotions) or pain points (such as layoffs) are allocated

- *Interpersonal fairness:* How well stakeholders are treated

- *Informational fairness:* Whether communication is honest and clear (in a 2011 study Jason Colquitt and Jessica Rodell found that this was the most important aspect for developing trust)

The French tire maker Michelin learned how important it is to have fair processes in 1999, when it decided to cut 7,500 jobs after posting a 17% increase in profits. The outrage in response to that move was so great that eventually the French prime minister outlawed subsidies for any business making layoffs without proof of financial duress.

So in 2003, when Michelin realized it would have to continue restructuring to remain competitive, the company decided it needed to find a better way. It spent the next decade developing new approaches to managing change in its manufacturing facilities.

The first strategy, called "ramp down and up," focused on shifting resources among plants—closing some while expanding others—as new products were brought on line and market needs evolved. Under this strategy, Michelin made every effort to keep affected employees in jobs at Michelin. The company would help them relocate to factories that were growing and provided support for the transition, such as assistance finding housing and information on the schools in their new towns. When relocation was not an option, Michelin would provide employees training in skills needed for jobs that were available locally and offer them professional counseling and support groups.

Success with the ramp-down-and-up approach led Michelin's leaders to later devise a bolder "turnaround" strategy, under which the management and employees of factories at risk of being shut down could propose detailed business plans to return them to profitability. If accepted, the plans would trigger investment from Michelin.

In carrying out these new approaches, the company demonstrated procedural, informational, interpersonal, and distributive fairness. In total it conducted 15 restructuring programs from 2003 to 2013, which included closing some plants while growing others and changing the mix of production capabilities among plants. But those reorganization efforts didn't get a lot of flack from the media, because the public didn't sound the alarm. In 2015, Michelin's first plant turnaround won the support of 95% of the factory's unionized workers. Michelin had demonstrated that it would use its power to treat employees fairly.

Does the company take responsibility for all its impact?

If stakeholders don't believe a company will produce positive effects, they'll limit its power. Part of the reason we have trouble forgiving Facebook is that its impact has been so enormous. The company might never have imagined that a hostile government would use its platform to influence an election or that a political consulting firm would harvest its users' data without their consent, but that's exactly what happened. And ultimately, what happens on Facebook's platform is seen as the responsibility of Facebook.

Wanting to generate beneficial effects isn't enough. Companies should carefully define the kind of impact they desire and then devise ways to measure and foster it. They must also have a plan for handling any unintended impact when it happens.

Pinterest, the social media platform, offers a good counterpoint to Facebook. Pinterest has very clearly defined the impact it wants to have on the world. Its mission statement reads: "Our mission is to help you discover and do what you love. That means showing you ideas that are relevant, interesting, and personal to you, and making sure you don't see anything that's inappropriate or spammy."

In extensive community guidelines, Pinterest details what it *doesn't* allow. For example, the company explains that it will "remove hate speech and discrimination, or groups and people that advocate either." Pinterest then elaborates: "Hate speech includes serious attacks on people based on their race, ethnicity, national origin, religion, gender identity, sexual orientation, disability or medical condition. Also, please don't target people based on their age, weight, immigration or veteran status."

The company trains reviewers to screen the content on its site to enforce its guidelines. Every six months it updates the training and guidelines, even though the process is time-consuming and expensive.

In fall of 2018, when people in the anti-vaccine movement chose to use the platform to spread their message, Pinterest took a simple yet effective step: It banned vaccination searches. Now if you search for vaccinations on the platform, nothing shows up. A few months later, Pinterest blocked accounts promoting fake cancer treatments and other nonscientifically vetted medical goods.

The company continues to work with outside experts to improve its ability to stop disinformation on its site. Pinterest understands that, given its estimated 250 million users, its platform could be both used and abused, and has taken action to ensure that it doesn't become a vehicle for causing harm.

How to Build and Rebuild Trust

Trust is less fragile than we think. Companies can be trusted in some ways but not others and still succeed. And trust can also be rebuilt.

Take the Japanese conglomerate Recruit Holdings. Its core businesses are advertising and online search and staffing, but its life-event platforms have transformed the way people find jobs, get married, and buy cars and houses, while its lifestyle platforms help customers book hair and nail appointments, make restaurant reservations, and take vacations.

From the beginning, Recruit designed its offerings around the principles of creating value and contributing to society. At the time it was launched, in 1960, large Japanese companies typically found new hires by hosting exams for job candidates at the top universities. Smaller companies that couldn't afford to host exams and students at other universities were shut out of the process. So Recruit's founder, Hiromasa Ezoe, started a magazine in which employers of all sizes could post job advertisements that could reach students at any university. Soon Recruit added such businesses as a magazine for selling secondhand cars and the first job-recruitment magazine aimed specifically at women.

However, in the 1980s, disaster struck the company. Ezoe was caught offering shares in a subsidiary to business, government, and media leaders before it went public. In all, 159 people were implicated in the scandal, and Japan's prime minister and his entire cabinet were forced to resign. A few years later one of Recruit's subsidiaries failed, saddling the company with annual interest payments that exceeded its annual income by ¥3 billion. Not long after that, Recruit suffered another major blow, when a main source of revenue, print advertising, was devastated by the rise of the internet.

This sequence of events would have easily felled another company, yet in 2018 Recruit had 40,000 employees and sales of $20 billion and operated in more than 60 countries. Today it's an internet giant, running 264 magazines (most online), some 200 websites, and 350 mobile apps. Despite its setbacks, Recruit continued to attract customers, nurture the best efforts of committed employees, and reward investors, and regained the respect of society.

To many executives, what Recruit pulled off sounds impossible. That may be because they subscribe to five popular myths that prevent people from understanding how to build and rebuild trust. Let's explore each of those myths and see how Recruit's experiences prove them wrong.

Myth: Trust has no boundaries
Reality: Trust is limited

Trust has three main components: the trusted party, the trusting party, and the action the trusted party is expected to perform. It's built by creating real but narrowly defined relationships.

Recruit was respected for its competence and, in particular, the way it trained its advertising salespeople to actively observe customers and come up with ways to make their businesses more successful. In the wake of the scandal, Recruit kept focusing on delivering the same high level of service. Because the stock violation didn't alter the company's ability to meet customers' expectations of competence, customers were willing to overlook it, and Recruit lost very few of them.

Myth: Trust is objective
Reality: Trust is subjective

Trust is based on the judgment of people and groups, not on some universal code of good conduct. If trust were a universal standard, Recruit's scandal would have led to its demise. However, even if society was outraged by the founder's actions (employees recalled that their children were embarrassed by their parents' jobs), customers still believed that Recruit's employees had their interests at heart. In time customers' trust led to increased profits, which made Recruit attractive to investors and society.

Myth: Trust is managed from the outside in—by controlling a firm's external image
Reality: Trust is managed from the inside out—by running a good business

All too often managers believe that improving a company's reputation is the work of advertising and PR firms or ever-vigilant online image-protection platforms. In actuality, reputation is an *output* that results when a company uses fair processes to deal with stakeholders. Be trustworthy and you will be trusted. Recruit had not only a track record for delivering good products and good service but a salesforce that was willing to work to save the company. Why? Because it had created a culture and systems that engaged and motivated employees. Employees wanted to save Recruit because they could not imagine a better place to work.

Recruit was built on the belief that employees do their best work when they discover a passion and learn to rely on themselves to pursue it. The company's motto is "Create your own opportunities and let the opportunities change you." Managers ask employees "Why are you here?" to help them invent projects that link their passions to a contribution to society. Here's how one employee in Recruit's Lifestyle Company recently described his project: "I'm involved with the development of a smartphone app. . . which helps men monitor their fertility and lower the obstacles they face in trying to conceive . . . . It is a real challenge to envision products that do not yet exist and make them real, but I am confident that in some small way my creative abilities can provide a service that will help people."

To ensure that all employees feel inspired by their work, Recruit makes them a unique offer: Once they reach the age of 35, they have the option of taking a $75,000 retirement bonus, providing they've been at Recruit at least six and a half years. The amount of the bonus increases as employees grow older. This offer is accompanied by career coaching that helps people make the right choice. People who have other dreams use the bonus to transition to different careers, making way for new employees with fresh perspectives on the needs of customers and society.

Myth: Companies are judged for their purpose
**Reality: Companies are judged for their purpose *and*
their impact**
Recruit's purpose had always been to add value to society. However,
that did not protect the company from fallout from the scandal.
Recruit was forced to take responsibility for the impact it had on the
country before it could regain people's trust. Because its senior managers understood this, they disregarded PR's dictate not to discuss
the scandal and told employees they could too. Kazuhiro Fujihara,
who was the head of sales at the time, explains: "I gathered my
employees and told them we could criticize the company for what
it had done. PR said we couldn't criticize the company, but I ignored
that." Today, Recruit has a section on its website describing the scandal, what it learned, and the actions it took to ensure that it would
not let something similar happen again. Recruit was well aware that
even though the scandal was caused by its founder, Ezoe's actions
were still its responsibility.

Myth: Trust is fragile. Once lost, it can never be regained
Reality: Trust waxes and wanes
More than three decades later, Recruit's stock scandal is still infa-
mous, but the company is thriving. The fall from grace was, Recruit
says on its website, "an opportunity to transform ourselves into a
new Recruit by encouraging each employee to confront the situation, think, make suggestions, and take action with a sense of owner-
ship rather than waiting passively based on the assumption that the
management team would rectify the situation. All proposals were
welcomed, including those concerning new business undertakings
and business improvements, provided they were forward looking."
That approach helped Recruit evolve and grow. It has expanded so
much internationally, in fact, that 46% of revenues now come from
outside Japan (up from 3.6% in 2011).

Now that we've broken down what trust is made of, let's put it all
together.

Building trust depends not on good PR but rather on clear purpose, smart strategy, and definitive action. It takes courage and common sense. It requires recognizing all the people and groups your company affects and focusing on serving their interests, not just your firm's. It means being competent, playing fair, and most of all, acknowledging and, if necessary, remediating, all the impact your company has, whether intended or not.

It's not always possible to make decisions that completely delight each of your stakeholder groups, but it is possible to make decisions that keep faith with and retain the trust they have in your company.

Originally published on July 16, 2019. Reprint H0512S

Customer Data: Designing for Transparency and Trust

by Timothy Morey, Theodore "Theo" Forbath, and Allison Schoop

WITH THE EXPLOSION OF DIGITAL TECHNOLOGIES, companies are sweeping up vast quantities of data about consumers' activities, both online and off. Feeding this trend are new smart, connected products—from fitness trackers to home systems—that gather and transmit detailed information.

Though some companies are open about their data practices, most prefer to keep consumers in the dark, choose control over sharing, and ask for forgiveness rather than permission. It's also not unusual for companies to quietly collect personal data they have no immediate use for, reasoning that it might be valuable someday.

As current and former executives at frog, a firm that helps clients create products and services that leverage users' personal data, we believe this shrouded approach to data gathering is shortsighted. Having free use of customer data may confer near-term advantages. But our research shows that consumers are aware that they're under surveillance—even though they may be poorly informed about the specific types of data collected about them—and are deeply anxious about how their personal information may be used.

In a future in which customer data will be a growing source of competitive advantage, gaining consumers' confidence will be key. Companies that are transparent about the information they gather, give customers control of their personal data, and offer fair value in return for it will be trusted and will earn ongoing and even expanded access. Those that conceal how they use personal data and fail to provide value for it stand to lose customers' goodwill—and their business.

The Expanding Scope of Data

The internet's first personal data collectors were websites and applications. By tracking users' activities online, marketers could deliver targeted advertising and content. More recently, intelligent technology in physical products has allowed companies in many industries to collect new types of information, including users' locations and behavior. The personalization this data allows, such as constant adaptation to users' preferences, has become central to the product experience. (Google's Nest thermostat, for example, autonomously adjusts heating and cooling as it learns homeowners' habits.)

The rich new streams of data have also made it possible to tackle complex challenges in fields such as health care, environmental protection, and urban planning. Take Medtronic's digital blood-glucose meter. It wirelessly connects an implanted sensor to a device that alerts patients and health care providers that blood-glucose levels are nearing troubling thresholds, allowing preemptive treatments. And the car service Uber has recently agreed to share ride-pattern data with Boston officials so that the city can improve transportation planning and prioritize road maintenance. These and countless other applications are increasing the power— and value—of personal data.

Of course, this flood of data presents enormous opportunities for abuse. Large-scale security breaches, such as the recent theft of the credit card information of 56 million Home Depot customers, expose

Idea in Brief

The Problem

Though consumers worry about how their personal data is gathered and used, they're surprisingly ignorant of what data they reveal when they're online, and most companies opt not to enlighten them. This dynamic erodes trust in firms and customers' willingness to share information.

The Solution

Companies need to design products and services with transparency and data privacy in mind. They must provide customers with appropriate value in exchange for data, educate them about how it is collected, and allow them to have control over it.

Best Practice

Disney devised electronic wristbands that give park visitors access to attractions and hotel rooms and allow them to charge food. Disney uses the bands to collect data on customers but clearly spells out its practices and privacy policies. The trade-offs are transparent to the customers, who find the convenience and other benefits the bands offer worthwhile.

consumers' vulnerability to malicious agents. But revelations about companies' covert activities also make consumers nervous. Target famously aroused alarm when it was revealed that the retailer used data mining to identify shoppers who were likely to be pregnant—in some cases before they'd told anyone.

At the same time, consumers appreciate that data sharing can lead to products and services that make their lives easier and more entertaining, educate them, and save them money. Neither companies nor their customers want to turn back the clock on these technologies—and indeed the development and adoption of products that leverage personal data continue to soar. The consultancy Gartner estimates that nearly 5 billion connected "things" will be in use in 2015—up 30% from 2014—and that the number will quintuple by 2020.

Resolving this tension will require companies and policy makers to move the data privacy discussion beyond advertising use and the simplistic notion that aggressive data collection is bad. We believe the answer is more nuanced guidance—specifically, guidelines that align the interests of companies and their customers, and ensure that both parties benefit from personal data collection.

Consumer Awareness and Expectations

To help companies understand consumers' attitudes about data, in 2014 we surveyed 900 people in five countries—the United States, the United Kingdom, Germany, China, and India—whose demographic mix represented the general online population. We looked at their awareness of how their data was collected and used, how they valued different types of data, their feelings about privacy, and what they expected in return for their data.

To find out whether consumers grasped what data they shared, we asked, "To the best of your knowledge, what personal information have you put online yourself, either directly or indirectly, by your use of online services?" While awareness varied by country—Indians are the most cognizant of their data trail and Germans the least—overall the survey revealed an astonishingly low recognition of the specific types of information tracked online. On average, only

In the dark about data

While most people are broadly aware that companies collect data on them, they're surprisingly uninformed about the specific types of data they give up when they go online.

Percentage of people who realize that they're sharing their:

27%	25%	23%	18%	17%	14%
Social network friends' list	Location	Web searches	Communication history (such as chat logs)	IP addresses	Web-surfing history

Putting a price on data

Surveys of consumers in the United States, China, India, Great Britain, and Germany reveal that they value some types of information much more highly than others.

Approximate amount people would pay to protect each data type (per person, US$, 2014)

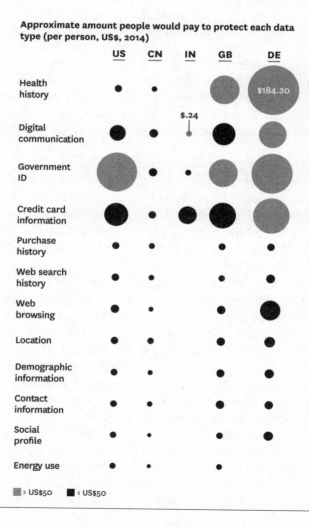

■ > US$50   ■ < US$50

25% of people knew that their data footprints included information on their location, and just 14% understood that they were sharing their web-surfing history too. (See the exhibit "In the dark about data.")

It's not as if consumers don't realize that data about them is being captured, however; 97% of the people surveyed expressed concern that businesses and the government might misuse their data. Identity theft was a top concern (cited by 84% of Chinese respondents at one end of the spectrum and 49% of Indians at the other). Privacy issues also ranked high; 80% of Germans and 72% of Americans are reluctant to share information with businesses because they "just want to maintain [their] privacy." So consumers clearly worry about their personal data—even if they don't know exactly what they're revealing.

To see how much consumers valued their data, we did conjoint analysis to determine what amount survey participants would be willing to pay to protect different types of information. (We used purchasing parity rather than exchange rates to convert all amounts to U.S. dollars.) Though the value assigned varied widely among individuals, we are able to determine, in effect, a median, by country, for each data type.

The responses revealed significant differences from country to country and from one type of data to another. (See the exhibit "Putting a price on data.") Germans, for instance, place the most value on their personal data, and Chinese and Indians the least, with British and American respondents falling in the middle. Government identification, health, and credit card information tended to be the most highly valued across countries, and location and demographic information among the least.

We don't believe this spectrum represents a "maturity model," in which attitudes in a country predictably shift in a given direction over time (say, from less privacy conscious to more). Rather, our findings reflect fundamental dissimilarities among cultures. The cultures of India and China, for example, are considered more hierarchical and collectivist, while Germany, the United

States, and the United Kingdom are more individualistic, which may account for their citizens' stronger feelings about personal information.

The Need to Deliver Value

If companies understand how much data is worth to consumers, they can offer commensurate value in return for it. Making the exchange transparent will be increasingly important in building trust.

A lot depends on the type of data and how the firm is going to use it. Our analysis looked at three categories: (1) *self-reported data*, or information people volunteer about themselves, such as their email addresses, work and educational history, and age and gender; (2) *digital exhaust*, such as location data and browsing history, which is created when using mobile devices, web services, or other connected technologies; and (3) *profiling data*, or personal profiles used to make predictions about individuals' interests and behaviors, which are derived by combining self-reported, digital exhaust, and other data. Our research shows that people value self-reported data the least, digital exhaust more, and profiling data the most.

We also examined three categories of data use: (1) *making a product or service better*, for example, by allowing a map application to recommend a route based on a user's location; (2) *facilitating targeted marketing or advertising*, such as ads based on a user's browsing history; and (3) *generating revenues through resale*, by, say, selling credit card purchase data to third parties.

Our surveys reveal that when data is used to improve a product or service, consumers generally feel the enhancement itself is a fair trade for their data. But consumers expect more value in return for data used to target marketing, and the most value for data that will be sold to third parties. In other words, the value consumers place on their data rises as its sensitivity and breadth increase from basic information that is voluntarily shared to detailed information about the consumer that the firm derives through analytics, and as its uses go from principally benefiting the consumer (in the form

Swapping value for data

The value people put on data rises as its breadth and sensitivity increase and its use shifts benefits toward companies. And the more people value data, the more they expect companies to provide in return for it.

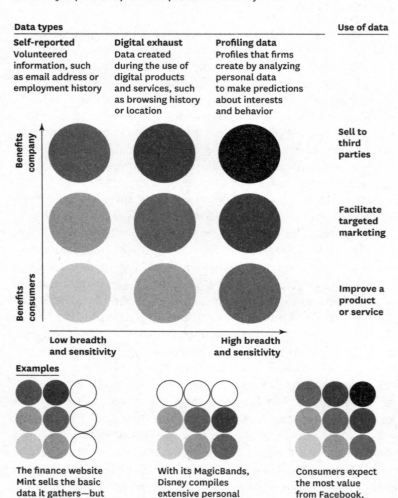

Data types

Self-reported
Volunteered information, such as email address or employment history

Digital exhaust
Data created during the use of digital products and services, such as browsing history or location

Profiling data
Profiles that firms create by analyzing personal data to make predictions about interests and behavior

Use of data

Sell to third parties

Facilitate targeted marketing

Improve a product or service

Benefits company

Benefits consumers

Low breadth and sensitivity

High breadth and sensitivity

Examples

The finance website Mint sells the basic data it gathers—but only to firms that can save consumers money.

With its MagicBands, Disney compiles extensive personal data but uses it only to improve service and advertising.

Consumers expect the most value from Facebook, which aggressively collects and sells all three kinds of data.

of product improvements) to principally benefiting the firm (in the form of revenues from selling data). (See the exhibit "Swapping value for data.")

Let's look now at how some companies manage this trade-off.

Samsung's Galaxy V smartphone uses digital exhaust to automatically add the contacts users call most to a favorites list. Most customers value the convenience enough to opt in to the feature—effectively agreeing to swap data for enhanced performance.

Google's predictive application Google Now harnesses profiling data to create an automated virtual assistant for consumers. By sifting through users' email, location, calendar, and other data, Google Now can, say, notify users when they need to leave the office to get across town for a meeting and provide a map for their commute. The app depends on more-valuable types of personal data but improves performance enough that many users willingly share it. Our global survey of consumers' attitudes toward predictive applications finds that about two-thirds of people are willing (and in some cases eager) to share data in exchange for their benefits.

Disney likewise uses profiling data gathered by its MagicBand bracelet to enhance customers' theme park and hotel experiences and create targeted marketing. By holding the MagicBand up to sensors around Disney facilities, wearers can access parks, check in at reserved attractions, unlock their hotel doors, and charge food and merchandise. Users hand over a lot of data, but they get convenience and a sense of privileged access in return, making the trade-off worthwhile. Consumers know exactly what they're signing on for, because Disney clearly spells out its data collection policies in its online MagicBand registration process, highlighting links to FAQs and other information about privacy and security.

Firms that sell personal information to third parties, however, have a particularly high bar to clear, because consumers expect the most value for such use of their data. The personal finance website Mint makes this elegant exchange: If a customer uses a credit card abroad and incurs foreign transaction fees, Mint flags the fees and refers the customer to a card that doesn't charge them. Mint receives a commission for the referral from the new-card issuer, and the customer avoids future fees. Mint and its customers both collect value from the deal.

Trust and Transparency

Firms may earn access to consumers' data by offering value in return, but trust is an essential facilitator, our research shows. The more trusted a brand is, the more willing consumers are to share their data.

Numerous studies have found that transparency about the use and protection of consumers' data reinforces trust. To assess this effect ourselves, we surveyed consumers about 46 companies representing seven categories of business around the world. We asked them to rate the firms on the following scale: *completely trustworthy* (respondents would freely share sensitive personal data with a firm because they trust the firm not to misuse it); *trustworthy* (they would "not mind" exchanging sensitive data for a desired service); *untrustworthy* (they would provide sensitive data only if required to do so in exchange for an essential service); and *completely untrustworthy* (they would never share sensitive data with the firm).

After primary care doctors, new finance firms such as PayPal and China's Alipay received the highest ratings on this scale, followed by e-commerce companies, consumer electronics makers, banks and insurance companies, and telecommunications carriers. Next came internet leaders (such as Google and Yahoo) and the government. Ranked below these organizations were retailers and entertainment companies, with social networks like Facebook coming in last. (See the exhibit "Do they trust you with their data?")

A firm that is considered untrustworthy will find it difficult or impossible to collect certain types of data, regardless of the value offered in exchange. Highly trusted firms, on the other hand, may be able to collect it simply by asking, because customers are satisfied with past benefits received and confident the company will guard their data. In practical terms, this means that if two firms offer the same value in exchange for certain data, the firm with the higher

Do they trust you with their data?

Consumers' faith that their personal information will be handled responsibly varies widely from industry to industry. Here are the percentages of people who said that each category of organization was "trustworthy" or "completely trustworthy" when it came to making sure that personal data was never used in any way that they wouldn't want.

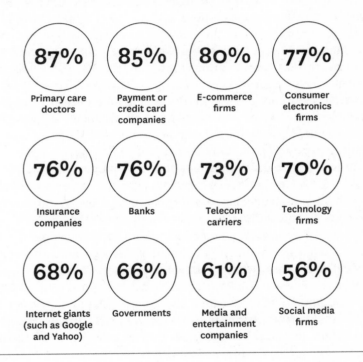

87% Primary care doctors

85% Payment or credit card companies

80% E-commerce firms

77% Consumer electronics firms

76% Insurance companies

76% Banks

73% Telecom carriers

70% Technology firms

68% Internet giants (such as Google and Yahoo)

66% Governments

61% Media and entertainment companies

56% Social media firms

trust will find customers more willing to share. For example, if Amazon and Facebook both wanted to launch a mobile wallet service, Amazon, which received good ratings in our survey, would meet with more customer acceptance than Facebook, which had low ratings. In this equation, trust could be an important competitive differentiator for Amazon.

Approaches That Build Trust

Many have argued that the extensive data collection today's business models rely on is fraught with security, financial, and brand risks. MIT's Sandy Pentland and others have proposed principles and practices that would give consumers a clear view of their data and control over its use, reducing firms' risks in the process. (See "With Big Data Comes Big Responsibility," HBR, November 2014.)

We agree that these business models are perilous and that risk reduction is essential. And we believe reasoned policies governing data use are important. But firms must also take the lead in educating consumers about their personal data. Any firm that thinks it's sufficient to simply provide disclosures in an end-user licensing agreement or present the terms and conditions of data use at sign-up is missing the point. Such moves may address regulatory requirements, but they do little if anything to help consumers.

Consider the belated trust-building efforts under way at Facebook. The firm has been accused of riding roughshod over user privacy in the past, launching services that pushed the boundaries on personal data use and retreating only in the face of public backlash or the threat of litigation. Facebook Beacon, which exposed users' web activities without their permission or knowledge, for example, was pulled only after a barrage of public criticism.

More recently, however, Facebook has increased its focus on safeguarding privacy, educating users, and giving them control. It grasps that trust is no longer just "nice to have." Commenting in a *Wired* interview on plans to improve Facebook Login, which allows users to log into third-party apps with their Facebook credentials, CEO Mark Zuckerberg explained that "to get to the next level and become more ubiquitous, [Facebook Login] needs to be trusted even more. We're a bigger company now and people have more questions. We need to give people more control over their information so that everyone feels comfortable using these products." In January 2015 Facebook launched Privacy Basics, an easy-to-understand site that explains what others see about a user and how people can customize and manage others' activities on their pages.

Using Humor to Teach About Data Privacy

Britain's Channel 4 does an excellent job of educating its viewers about its data collection and privacy policy. On a dedicated website, the TV station details the type of information gathered and how it's used, and summarizes the policy in a short, entertaining video with comedian Alan Carr. As he deadpans, "We'll ask you for your name, email, and a few other details. Now, I know what you're thinking. Why should you give us your name and inside-leg measurement? What will we do with that information?" He then explains that viewers maintain complete control of their data, that it will never be sold, and that it can be erased from the system at their request at any time.

The video, which has been watched millions of times, is one component of Channel 4's vigorous Viewer Promise program. According to Steven Forde, the channel's director of viewer relationship management, these efforts have built trust and encouraged data sharing: Eleven million viewers have registered on the site. Eighty percent of them volunteer their address details, though they're not required to, and fewer than 0.01% opt out of targeted advertising.

Like Facebook, Apple has had its share of data privacy and security challenges—most recently when celebrity iPhoto accounts were hacked—and is taking those concerns ever more seriously. Particularly as Apple forays into mobile payments and watch-based fitness monitoring, consumer trust in its data handling will be paramount. CEO Tim Cook clearly understands this. Launching a "bid to be conspicuously transparent," as the *Telegraph* put it, Apple recently introduced a new section on its website devoted to data security and privacy. At the top is a message from Cook. "At Apple, your trust means everything to us," he writes. "That's why we respect your privacy and protect it with strong encryption, plus strict policies that govern how all data is handled . . . . We believe in telling you up front exactly what's going to happen to your personal information and asking for your permission before you share it with us."

On the site, Apple describes the steps taken to keep people's location, communication, browsing, health tracking, and transactions private. Cook explains, "Our business model is very straightforward: We sell great products. We don't build a profile based on your email content or web browsing habits to sell to advertisers. We don't 'monetize' the information you store on your iPhone or in iCloud. And we don't read your email or your messages to get information to market to you. Our software and services are designed to make our devices better. Plain and simple." Its new stance earned Apple the highest possible score—six stars—from the nonprofit digital rights organization Electronic Frontier Foundation, a major improvement over its 2013 score of one star.

Enlightened Data Principles

Facebook and Apple are taking steps in the right direction but are fixing issues that shouldn't have arisen in the first place. Firms in that situation start the trust-building process with a handicap. Forward-looking companies, in contrast, are incorporating data privacy and security considerations into product development from the start, following three principles. The examples below each highlight one principle, but ideally companies should practice all three.

Teach your customers

Users can't trust you if they don't understand what you're up to. Consider how one of our clients educates consumers about its use of highly sensitive personal data.

This client, an information exchange for biomedical researchers, compiles genomic data on anonymous participants from the general public. Like all health information, such data is highly sensitive and closely guarded. Building trust with participants at the outset is essential. So the project has made education and informed consent central to their experience. Before receiving a kit for collecting a saliva sample for analysis, volunteers must watch a video about the potential consequences of having their genome sequenced— including the possibility of discrimination in employment and insurance—and after viewing it, must give a preliminary online consent to the process. The kit contains a more detailed hard-copy agreement that, once signed and returned with the sample, allows the exchange to include the participant's anonymized genomic information in the database. If a participant returns the sample without the signed consent, her data is withheld from the exchange. Participants can change their minds at any time, revoking or granting access to their data.

Give them control
The principle of building control into data exchange is even more fully developed in another project, the Metadistretti e-monitor, a collaboration between frog, Flextronics, the University Politecnico di Milano, and other partners. Participating cardiac patients wear an e-monitor, which collects ECG data and transmits it via smartphone to medical professionals and other caregivers. The patients see all their own data and control how much data goes to whom, using a browser and an app. They can set up networks of health care providers, of family and friends, or of fellow users and patients, and send each different information. This patient-directed approach is a radical departure from the tradition of paternalistic medicine that carries over to many medical devices even today, with which the patient doesn't own his data or even have access to it.

Deliver in-kind value
Businesses needn't pay users for data (in fact, our research suggests that offers to do so actually reduce consumers' trust). But as we've discussed, firms do have to give users value in return.

The music service Pandora was built on this principle. Pandora transparently gathers self-reported data; customers volunteer their age, gender, and zip code when they sign up, and as they use the service they tag the songs they like or don't like. Pandora takes that information and develops a profile of each person's musical tastes so that it can tailor the selection of songs streamed to him or her; the more data users provide, the better the tailoring becomes. In the free version of its service, Pandora uses that data to target advertising. Customers get music they enjoy at no charge and ads that are more relevant to them. Consumers clearly find the trade satisfactory; the free service has 80 million active subscribers.

In designing its service, Pandora understood that customers are most willing to share data when they know what value they'll receive in return. It's hard to set up this exchange gracefully, but one effective approach is to start slowly, asking for a few pieces of low-value data that can be used to improve a service. Provided that there's a clear link between the data collected and the enhancements delivered, customers will become more comfortable sharing additional data as they grow more familiar with the service.

———————

If your company still needs another reason to pursue the data principles we've described, consider this: Countries around the world are clamping down on businesses' freewheeling approach to personal data.

There is an opportunity for companies in this defining moment. They can abide by local rules only as required, or they can help lead the change under way. Grudging and minimal compliance may keep a firm out of trouble but will do little to gain consumers' trust—and may even undermine it. Voluntarily identifying and adopting the most stringent data privacy policies will inoculate a firm against legal challenges and send consumers an important message that helps confer competitive advantage. After all, in an information economy, access to data is critical, and consumer trust is the key that will unlock it.

Originally published in May 2015. Reprint R1505H

Operational Transparency

by Ryan W. Buell

BARCLAYS BANK INSTALLED the world's first successful automated teller machine to much fanfare in June 1967. Having a machine distribute cash was less expensive and more efficient than having a human teller do it. What's more, customers could access the ATM at any hour—even when the bank was closed. It seemed like a win-win, and ATMs quickly spread around the world. Today people are three times more likely to withdraw money from an ATM than from a human teller.

However, there's a wrinkle to the ATM success story. When customers use ATMs more and tellers less, their overall level of satisfaction with their bank goes down. It turns out that when consumers can't see the work that's being done to serve them, their perception is that less effort went into delivering the service, so they don't appreciate or value it as much. ATMs carry out complex work: They reliably identify customers, find their account information, and then accurately complete the transaction—all while protecting the confidentiality of their private information. But separated from this work by a hard, metallic surface and a vague "processing transaction" message, customers take the "wizardry" for granted in a way that they don't when they're face-to-face with tellers who are working in their behalf.

Automation has enabled enormous efficiencies in recent years, but it has also detached customers from operations. Thanks to fleets of order-picking robots and miles of automated conveyors, it takes less than one minute of human labor to pick, pack, and ship the typical Amazon package—a miraculous ballet among people and machines that customers never glimpse. Google has more than a million servers working to deliver answers to more than a trillion queries a year—information distributed in fractions of a second without a hint of the massive operation behind it.

And even where technology hasn't erected barriers between customers and the work being performed for them, leaders have put them up. At hospitals, as many as 70% of clinical diagnoses come from the pathology lab—but the people who run those tests are often hidden away in the basement or off-site. Hundreds of people have a hand in the successful takeoff and landing of a commercial flight—but for the most part, passengers see only the cabin crew. Consider all the people who work in offices, kitchens, warehouses, and factories whose efforts create immeasurable value but who never enter customers' minds.

Therein lies a crucial managerial dilemma that I've been studying over the past decade. It has long been believed that the more contact an operation has with its customers, the less efficiently it runs. Customers are, as a researcher in the 1960s boldly called them, "environmental disturbances." As the argument goes, separating customers from internal processes through physical distance, time, or the introduction of technology enables companies to perform more efficiently and, in turn, create more value for consumers. But my research shows that the pendulum can swing too far. When customers are cordoned off from a company's operation, they are less likely to fully understand and appreciate the value being created. As a result, they are less satisfied, less willing to pay, less trusting, and less loyal to the company over time. Employees also suffer when they are cut off from the business's front lines, as they lose the motivation and enjoyment that comes from making a difference in people's lives and are denied the opportunities to learn and improve that arise from interaction with customers.

One solution that my colleagues and I have investigated is the introduction of operational transparency—the deliberate design of

Idea in Brief

The Dilemma

Conventional wisdom holds that the more contact an operation has with its customers, the less efficiently it will run. But when customers are partitioned away from the operation, they are less likely to fully understand and appreciate the work going on behind the scenes, thereby placing a lower value on the product or service being offered.

The Solution

Managers should experiment with operational transparency—the deliberate design of windows into and out of the organization's operations to help customers understand and appreciate the value being added.

The Benefits

Witnessing the hidden work performed on their behalf makes customers more satisfied, more willing to pay, and more loyal. It can also make employees more satisfied by demonstrating to them that they are serving their customers well. However, managers should be aware of certain conditions in which transparency can backfire.

---

windows into and out of the organization's operations to help customers and employees alike understand and appreciate the value being created. To determine when and how to design such windows, managers must understand when and how customers and employees want to open up operations to scrutiny—and when both parties would prefer that work be undertaken behind the scenes.

Behind the Curtain

I first started documenting the beneficial effects of operational transparency in 2008, when I set up a mock website called Travel Finder, with my Harvard Business School colleague Michael Norton, as part of a study. We had noticed that travel agents, like bank tellers, were being made increasingly obsolete by technology—in this case, by online travel agencies. We also noticed that most online ticket sites hid the work they performed for customers behind progress bars and activity spinners, or behind marketing messages such as "Did you know you can book your hotel with us, too?" Online travel agency Kayak was an exception. The company showed customers how many different airlines it was searching while they waited, and it slotted itineraries into the results screen as they were found instead of all at once. We wondered whether this operational transparency would change the way customers viewed the service.

For our travel study, we recruited people to search for flights from Boston to Los Angeles on our website. After they entered their search information, we randomly varied how long people waited as the website searched for possible tickets. While waiting, some people saw a progress bar, and some were shown, in addition to the progress bar, the hidden work that the website was doing: "Now getting results from American Airlines . . . from JetBlue . . . 133 results found so far . . . Now 427 . . ." We then surveyed people about how valuable they perceived the website to be. No matter how long people had waited, they always considered the website to be more valuable when it showed the work it was doing for them. They also reported a higher willingness to pay, a perception of higher quality, and a greater desire to use the site again. What's more, they were also considerably less sensitive to their wait time when they experienced operational transparency. People who received instantaneous service perceived the service to be as valuable as people who waited 25 seconds with a progress bar, and as valuable as people who waited 55 seconds with operational transparency. That's remarkable in an era in which we have come to expect online services to be delivered in fractions of a second.

In other experiments, people who experienced operational transparency expressed more interest in using the website again in the future, even when they compared it with a faster website that returned the same results and did not show the work. We also found that people preferred websites that showed them the work over ones that did other things to distract from the wait—like providing entertaining pictures of their destination, promotional messages about other services offered by the website, or an interactive game of tic-tac-toe. None of those types of approaches made the service seem more valuable.

Why does operational transparency seem to have this unique power? We surveyed people who have (and have not) been given a glimpse behind the curtain in services as varied as restaurants, retail, and online dating to learn how operational transparency changes their perceptions. We found that when people could see the work that was going on behind the scenes, they perceived that more effort went into the delivery of the service. They also believed that the service provider had more expertise and was being more thorough. They appreciated that effort and quality, and they in turn valued the service more.

In retail, for instance, Bhavya Mohan (of the University of San Francisco), Leslie John (of Harvard Business School), and I studied what happened when an online retailer added an infographic highlighting the costs and processes involved in manufacturing various products. For example, a wallet that sold for $115.00 included costs for raw materials ($14.68), construction ($38.56), duties ($4.26), and transportation ($1.00). Revealing the costs enabled the company to showcase to customers the otherwise hidden work that went into creating the wallet. In the process, of course, it also revealed that customers were paying $115.00 for something that cost $58.50 to make. The company further informed customers that its 1.9x markup compared favorably with the 6x markup charged by competing retailers—whose prices for similarly constructed items were higher. We found that sales of the wallets with operational transparency went up by 26% relative to wallets where the costs were not shared.

In subsequent experiments, we've learned that voluntarily providing operational transparency not only increases sales but also increases people's trust and satisfaction—even in settings where trust is otherwise low, such as government services. According to the Pew Research Center, 73% of Americans in 1958 reported trusting government to do the right thing at least most of the time; today a paltry 20% do. So-called sunshine laws require a minimum level of transparency by elected officials and policy makers about certain of their activities, but those laws are not meant to spotlight the often invisible work that government does on a daily basis to create value in citizens' lives—such as disposing of trash, filling potholes, cleaning up graffiti, and fixing broken streetlights.

In 2009, Boston's local government developed a smartphone app called Citizens Connect (now BOS:311), which enables residents of the city to submit public service requests. Using the app, a resident can take a photo of a problem they want to report, such as a pothole, and the picture will automatically be geotagged using the phone's GPS and sent to the public works department. My colleagues Ethan Porter (of George Washington University), Michael Norton (of HBS), and I partnered with the City of Boston and Code for America in 2014 to study how showing the work being performed affected people's perceptions of government. We found that when people interacted with a website that showed images of the work being requested and performed, they became significantly more trusting and supportive of the government than if they interacted with a website that merely provided a tally of issues being reported and resolved. What's more, when the city took things a step further and asked employees to take photos of the work they were doing and share them with the people who submitted the original requests, users became considerably more engaged, increasing the number of requests they made on a monthly basis by 60% and reporting issues in 40% more categories. Increased citizen engagement enabled Boston's government to allocate more workers to solving problems and fewer to finding them, so more work could get done.

The thoughtful application of transparency can create value even in settings where privacy is traditionally prized, such as health care. London Business School's Kamalini Ramdas and Nazli Sonmez and I collaborated with doctors at Aravind Eye Hospital, in Pondicherry, India, to study an application of operational transparency in delivering care to patients with glaucoma—an eye disease that is the second leading cause of blindness and afflicts some 12 million Indians. Some patients in our study were given appointments with their doctors in accordance with the hospital's normal protocol. Others were given shared appointments with three or four other patients. At the shared appointments, patients were able to see what the doctor could see when examining the eyes of others and hear the questions asked by other patients. Results from our ongoing collaboration suggest that patients who have shared medical appointments are more satisfied and engaged during their experience, are more likely to ask questions, learn more from the interactions, are more compliant with their pre-scriptions, and are more likely to return for follow-up care than patients who have traditional one-on-one appointments with their doctor.

Although companies generally strive to make services appear as effortless as possible, examples of organizations beginning to experiment with various forms of operational transparency are becoming more abundant. When customers use an ATM to withdraw money from their BBVA bank accounts in Spain, the ATM's full-color screen displays visual representations of the currency being counted, sorted, and arranged for distribution. At most Starbucks drive-through locations in the United States, the intercom has been replaced with a video monitor and camera system. When customers place an order, they come face-to-face with the barista as he or she rings up the order and marks instructions on each cup. At Domino's, customers can use the company's Pizza Tracker app to watch as the kitchen workers prep, bake, and package the pizza for delivery.

NPR and the *New York Times* podcast *The Daily* are connecting listeners and readers with the otherwise obscure work involved in researching, producing, and delivering the headlines of the day. NPR posts live feeds from its studios, and *The Daily* interviews the paper's own reporters. In Detroit, the Mayor's Office has invested in the Neighborhood Improvement Tracker, a public-facing website that shows at a lot-by-lot level the many efforts being directed toward the city's recovery, such as demolitions scheduled and completed to remove urban blight and building permits issued to enhance the community.

The evidence is clear: Operational transparency can fundamentally reshape the ways customers understand, perceive, and engage with the organizations that serve them. But what of employees?

Closing the Loop for Employees

Pioneering studies of service industries in the early 2000s found that a primary driver of satisfaction among employees is the knowledge that their company is delivering results to happy customers. Indeed, a 2007 study led by Adam Grant, an organizational psychologist and professor at Wharton, found that when call center agents soliciting donations for college scholarships actually met some of the students their work supported, their productivity and persistence skyrocketed. But what happens when the interaction between the customer and employee occurs in real time?

In 2012, Tami Kim (of the Darden School of Business), Chia-Jung Tsay (of University College London), and I ran an experiment in the Annenberg Hall dining facility at Harvard, which serves more than 3,000 meals every day. Annenberg was built in the late 1800s at a time when it was considered uncouth for diners to be able to see the work taking place in the kitchen. In that tradition, diners at Annenberg who desire eggs, a fish sandwich, a hamburger, or some other grill item cooked their way must write their order on a piece of paper and hand it to an employee, who passes it through a small window into the kitchen, where a chef reads the order, cooks the item, and places it back in the window to be taken by an employee and given to the customer. The chefs can't see the customers, and the customers can't see the chefs.

We installed iPads with videoconferencing software—one at the order station, in view of the customers, and another in the kitchen, in view of the chefs. We then timed how long it took to make various dishes and measured both chef and diner satisfaction. When we turned on the iPads in a way that allowed only the chefs to see their customers, customer satisfaction with the food rose 14%. When we turned on the iPads so the customers could see the chefs too, satisfaction went up 22%, and the chefs worked 19% faster. One chef told us, "When [the customers] can see us [make their food], they appreciate it, and I appreciate that. It makes me want to improve."

Through surveys and additional experiments, we learned that when customers saw the chefs cooking their food, they perceived that more effort went into serving them, they appreciated the effort, and they valued the service more. When the chefs could see their customers—the people who were benefiting from their efforts—the work they were doing seemed more appreciated and impactful, making them more satisfied with their jobs and more willing to exert effort. It was a virtuous cycle.

Consider another example: the Japanese train-cleaning company, Tessei, which I researched with Ethan Bernstein for an HBS case study. Tessei is charged with the Herculean task of cleaning the Shinkansen bullet trains during their brief stops at Tokyo station—1,000 seats in seven minutes. That's the equivalent of cleaning six Boeing 737s in less than half the time it typically takes to clean one. In the early 2000s, Tessei's employees were struggling to get the job done. Part of the challenge was that the work was underappreciated: Cleaning the bullet trains was known to be dirty and difficult, and so being a cleaner at Tessei was considered shameful in Japan. Accordingly, workers did whatever they could to escape the notice of customers. In 2005, a new leader, Teruo Yabe, revitalized the service, in part by promoting operational transparency among customers and employees. After the company changed employee uniforms from an invisible pale blue (which blended in with the body of the trains) to a vibrant red, passengers began to see and appreciate the work that these crews were doing, and after more interaction was instituted between the workers and the passengers, employees felt more appreciated and found a greater sense of purpose in their work. Employees began suggesting process improvements, and customers began chipping in to help tidy up their seats. There were quantifiable performance improvements too; today a Tessei crew can clean a train in four minutes.

The India-based luxury hotel chain Oberoi Hotels takes operational transparency one step further, as I learned in my research for an HBS case study with Ananth Raman (of HBS) and Vidhya Muthuram (of the Blavatnik School of Government). Every employee in the company is preauthorized to spend up to Rs 1,500 (about US$25) to create moments of delight for guests. Whenever they learn of an opportunity to customize the service to improve a guest's experience, they're encouraged to act on it. The only stipulation is that employees must log what they have done so that the company and other employees can learn from their creativity. What has resulted is a feedback loop that fosters in employees a greater sense of purpose, helps customers feel better cared for, and improves organizational learning. Thanks in part to these efforts, Oberoi's properties routinely receive effusive reviews in customer surveys, and the company is perennially rated as one of the best luxury hotel brands in the world.

In contexts in which designing a face-to-face connection between employees and customers is impractical, technology can be used to successfully facilitate operational transparency. In 2013, Domino's piloted a feature called Domino's Live in one of its Salt Lake City locations, installing web cameras in the kitchen. Building on its Pizza Tracker app, customers ordering pizzas in Salt Lake could log on and watch a live feed of their pizzas being made. As it turned out, tens of thousands of people from around the country logged on to watch other people's pizzas get made. Recognizing the potential, Domino's promoted Domino's Live on Facebook, and anytime someone clicked the "Like" button, a "Like Light" in the kitchen went on. This gave the pizza makers a signal that someone looking on appreciated the work they were doing. Although Domino's discontinued Domino's Live, the company added a feature to Pizza Tracker that enables customers to send notes of encouragement through the app to the people who are preparing their pizzas—prespecified messages such as "I don't know what I'd do without you" and "You are my pizza-making heroes." In a similar move, Uber recently updated its app to allow riders to close the loop with drivers—prompting them to send thank-you notes, along with tips, to the drivers after the ride is over. As one driver explained, "It makes my day to know when I've made somebody else's."

The Risk of Backfire

For all its benefits, operational transparency doesn't always deliver positive results. There are circumstances when it can repel customers and undermine employees. But even in such instances, managers should think twice before opting for complete opacity. Operational transparency should be carefully considered when:

It reveals things people genuinely don't want to see
Few may desire a behind-the-scenes look at trash collection or enjoying watching the dashcam footage of a violent police altercation.

However, there's a difference between transparency that elicits the reaction "I'd rather not see that" and transparency that elicits the reaction "That should not happen." In the case of services that people aren't really interested in or find unappealing, companies should look for ways to use transparency to change the way people think about and engage with a service. For example, the city of Halifax, Nova Scotia, switched to clear trash bags in 2015 so that everyone could see what was being thrown away. Curbside waste collection fell by more than 30%, and recycling rates increased nearly 20%. When transparency causes people to object to what they see, organizations can draw on the experience to come up with alternative approaches that improve practice going forward. Dashcam footage of excessive violence by police departments has led to public outrage, but it has also improved oversight and accountability, sparked conversations that have led to policy change, and improved frontline training. "Out of sight, out of mind" may be more comfortable for everyone in the moment, but it rarely ensures the best long-term outcomes.

It engenders anxiety

Showing customers every step while their credit is being evaluated for a loan, or peering over employees' shoulders as they work, amplifies anxiety. Ethan Bernstein, of HBS, found that when curtains were put up around production lines at a Chinese cell phone manufacturer, productivity increased by 10% to 15%. Free from prying eyes, workers felt more focused and licensed to experiment with ways to improve standardized processes. What's more, workers felt safe to share ideas with one another, building team camaraderie and improving performance. When transparency makes us feel watched, it can hold us back; but when it helps us feel engaged, it can move us forward. For example, my HBS colleague Michelle Shell and I found that when customers who were transparently being evaluated for a loan were also provided with an easy way to contact a support person with questions throughout the process, the probability they would move forward with the loan, if offered, increased.

It shatters our faith in the relationship

When transparency reveals that a company isn't even-handed or that its practices violate implicit social norms, it makes customers understandably upset. Incidents of air rage—when an irate passenger causes a plane to land early—are higher on flights that have both a business class and an economy class and all passengers board from the front, forcing people in economy class to experience the disparity. This study, conducted by Katherine DeCelles (of the Rotman School of Management) and Michael Norton, found that when the plane boards in the middle, so there's less transparency, the effect goes away. Or consider the ubiquitous marketing practice of personalizing ads. Tami Kim, along with Kate Barasz (of HBS) and Leslie John, found that when companies are transparent about targeting online ads on the basis of things we've revealed about ourselves, we appreciate the personalization. But when the transparency instead shows that they customize ads according to things they've *inferred* about us, it makes us upset. Customers also bristle when it's clear instead that companies are sharing their information with third parties without permission.

It destroys the magic

Sometimes we want to suspend our disbelief, and providing too much transparency would make that impossible. Retailers that sell high-end jewelry, musical instruments, or home decor often keep redundant inventory off the floor to give the pieces we see a special, one-of-a-kind mystique. The illusion that our ring or guitar or vase is unique enhances our experience. Likewise, even when it's 95 degrees outside, the cast member playing Mickey Mouse at Disneyland should keep the heavy, stuffy head of the costume on during the parade. Nothing can ruin the experience of make-believe like too much transparency. In other cases, we're fascinated to be in on the secret. Factory tours and "how it's made" shows are ubiquitous, and we clamor to watch bloopers and outtakes from our favorite movies. In fact, Disney offers a Backstage Magic experience for those who self-select into peeking behind the curtain.

It exposes an ineffective process

When transparency reveals employees who are incapable, indifferent, or powerless to deliver on the value proposition of the firm, customers can become incensed. Think back to the last service interaction you had where two employees were visibly chatting with each other instead of helping you. Or remember the last time your simmering frustration rose to a boil when a customer service rep repeated apologies for a problem over and over but had no means or authority to remedy the situation. Meanwhile, exposing employees to disenchanted and overtly negative customers, whom they have no hope of satisfying, can be a recipe for burnout. Agent turnover in many call centers, for example, exceeds 150% per year. Often situations like these arise when transparency hasn't been designed to be reciprocal and to engender learning. Transparency that is accompanied by mechanisms to collect and learn from customer-provided feedback can accelerate, and create opportunities to celebrate, improvement.

It reveals that a company's best efforts yield poor results

When people can see that a lot of behind-the-scenes effort went into creating an inadequate outcome, it reinforces their impression that the company is bad at what it does. In an experiment I conducted with Michael Norton, participants engaged with one of two online dating websites that gave them dissatisfying results. Participants perceived that the site that showed them how hard it was working was worse than the one that delivered the same bad result but didn't show the work. The impression was, "You tried so hard, and that's the best you could do? You must not be very good at your job." That said, when mistakes are made, timely transparency is still typically the best path. Customers may punish companies that fail to be transparent about missteps or errors, questioning the organization's motives for hiding the information. "Why did Equifax wait 40 days to inform 143 million people that their confidential information had been compromised?" customers might wonder. Or "Why did Facebook wait three years to disclose that Cambridge Analytica improperly accessed the records of 50 million users?"

It shows that the company's products or services are inferior to competitors'

A fundamental tenet of business still applies: If your customers find that your products are of poor quality, overly expensive, or otherwise less attractive than your competitors' offerings, they will do business elsewhere. Shwetha Mariadassou (of Stanford), Yanchong Zheng (of MIT), and I found that such revelations are most damaging when a company's level of performance is seen as inferior to a competitor or industry benchmark. On the other hand, transparency that exposes a customer's own poor performance—for example, when your power company reports that you consume more electricity than your neighbors—can be a potent motivator of change. The effect can be especially powerful when the company reveals unflattering changes in your performance: You increased consumption by 5%, but your neighbors decreased consumption by an average of 3%.

It highlights a lack of progress

Uncertainty about our status makes our skin crawl. That's why progress bars are ubiquitous online, and why American, Delta, and United Airlines now update the status of people's bags throughout their journey, providing mobile alerts when bags have been scanned, loaded, off-loaded, placed in baggage claim, and so on. We like to have the feeling of moving forward, and transparency that demonstrates the opposite can be frustrating. For example, in a recent experiment, I found that when people who have been waiting for service can see that nobody has joined the queue behind them, they're significantly more likely to give up waiting than if they don't know whether anyone else has joined. Making visible their lack of progress from the end of the queue leaves them wondering whether continuing to wait is worthwhile. On the other hand, when people who have been waiting for service are able to see that their time waiting has resulted in advancement from the end of the queue, they're significantly more likely to stay in line.

It reveals that the company's operations harm workers or the environment

News coverage of the 2013 collapse of Rana Plaza, which killed and injured thousands of Bangladeshi garment workers, and the 2010 Deepwater Horizon oil spill, which released millions of barrels of oil into the Gulf of Mexico, casts spotlights on inhumane working conditions and subpar environmental standards that reshaped corporate initiatives around supply chain sustainability. Visibility into such problems can cause a strong and swift customer backlash. To that end, transparency functions as a test of sorts: If you don't want people to see how you treat your employees or the planet, you probably need to make some changes. On the other hand, when transparency reveals that companies are operating sustainably, it can have a powerful effect.

Georgia Institute of Technology's Basak Kalkanci and I ran field experiments with Alta Gracia, an apparel manufacturer that pays a living wage to its workers in the Dominican Republic, and with Counter Culture Coffee, a North Carolina–based coffee roasting company that engages in environmentally sustainable practices. We collaborated with the Looma Project to produce a short video showing footage of working conditions inside Alta Gracia's factory and featuring interviews with workers discussing the living wage that Alta Gracia pays. We produced a similar video highlighting Counter Culture Coffee's environmental sustainability practices, such as composting the chaff from its roasting process to reduce landfill waste. Showing these videos at point-of-sale kiosks increased the probability that customers would buy the company's products by roughly 20%, relative to merely showing brand videos.

It's deceptive

Transparency is helpful when it reveals work, but when the illusion of transparency is used to deceive or manipulate, it can backfire spectacularly. When customers call AT&T or Apple to request customer support, the companies' automated systems play the sound of typing between prompts to signal that work is being done. Customers understand these cues for what they are and do not mistake them for the sound of an actual person performing a task. However, companies can easily stray into dodgy territory. For example, several years ago, a company called Premier Health Plans used software to speak on behalf of telemarketing agents who had heavy accents. Calls would typically start off with the agent identifying "herself" as Samantha West and asking an initial question, prompting customers to think they were engaging with a live customer service rep. However, awkward pauses between exchanges, the software's limited repertoire of phrases, and the mechanical word-for-word repetition that resulted during interactions caused skeptical customers to interrupt, asking, "Are you a robot?" Anticipating this possibility, the developers had included the recording of a disarming laugh and the response "I am a real person. Can you hear me OK?" Customers weren't buying it. Recordings soon emerged online of people interrogating Samantha West to expose her as a fraud.

Recently, Google announced its plans to roll out a much more sophisticated phone robot, called Google Duplex, that is fully automated and can pass as a human—calling restaurants and hair salons to make reservations and appointments on behalf of its users. The technology is breathtaking, and the potential for value creation is enormous, but unless Duplex is modified to be genuinely transparent, it's hard to imagine that those it deceives will be forgiving.

Bringing Operational Transparency to Your Organization

Given all the potential advantages and pitfalls of operational transparency, managers should be thoughtful about how they implement it. They should consider the following factors in designing their initiatives:

What to reveal?

A great place to start is to think about moments in the process that could be easily showcased with minimal effort. For example, one dessert-focused restaurant introduced operational transparency by suspending a tilted mirror from the ceiling above the pastry chefs who were plating and finishing desserts. Diners, whose views had been previously obscured by high counters and a bank of espresso machines, were captivated by their new window into the action.

Other opportunities for transparency can be found by considering what information already captured in the organization's databases would be appreciated by customers. For example, several years ago, as a part of its efforts to improve access to health care, the U.S. Department of Veterans Affairs began internally tracking how long veterans were waiting at each of its facilities to get an appointment to see a doctor. Recently, the agency made this information publicly available to patients on its website. Similarly, Quick Lane Tire and Auto Center, a nationwide auto repair company, has been experimenting with providing a digital information board in its waiting rooms that gives customers real-time updates about what's happening with their cars and the current status of the service queue.

When to reveal?

Transparency boosts value perceptions most when it reveals work as it is happening or just after it has been completed, rather than showing work that has not yet occurred. In my research, I've found that customers are more satisfied when a travel site like Kayak shows its efforts to find a flight *as it searches* dozens of airlines than when it merely tells customers before they hit the "search" button *that it will search* dozens of airlines. In addition, consumers shouldn't be force-fed transparency. Rather, they should get to decide when they want to see more. For example, UPS receives 143 million package-tracking requests on a typical business day—which converts to an average of about seven lookups per package. These requests are made by customers who are actively curious about the status of particular packages and are tracking them at times of their choosing. Imagine if UPS instead called you at its own discretion seven times per shipment with a running progress report.

How to reveal?

Transparency implementations work best when they're visual— ideally giving customers actual windows into the process so that there's no question about the credibility of what's being shown.

When this isn't possible, video or animated infographics and diagrams that provide a visual representation of the work boost the perception of value more than static imagery, which in turn outperforms text descriptions. Transparency also works best when it's voluntarily provided by companies; transparency that is wrung out of corporations as a result of regulations, investor pressure, or other factors does not build trust.

Don't forget to close the loop. Transparency is the most beneficial when it's allowed to flow in both directions—from the customers into the operation and from the employees out to the customers. Forcing employees to toil in obscurity deprives them of seeing how their work is helping customers, reducing their feeling that their work is appreciated and undermining their motivation. What's more, transparency for employees can give them the information they need to customize service and help them learn better ways of operating.

In a sense, today's businesses have become victims of the global economy's immense productivity gains over the past two centuries. Consumers today rely on a dizzying array of products that are manufactured and distributed from all around the world and on services that are delivered with an intensifying frequency. But the apparently effortless abundance and convenience also make it easy for consumers to take work for granted and for employees to lose out on the learning and motivation that customer connections afford. With that in mind, businesses should stop reflexively hiding their operations for the sake of efficiency and instead thoughtfully consider when and how to open them up to create more value for customers and employees alike.

Originally published in March–April 2019. Reprint R1902H

Disclosure: Ryan W. Buell has given paid lectures at Google and Uber in the past.

The Organizational Apology

by Maurice E. Schweitzer, Alison Wood Brooks, and Adam D. Galinsky

THE *WASHINGTON POST* called it "creepy." The *Atlantic* said it "might have been illegal." One privacy advocate wondered if it could have made people suicidal.

Those were just some of the reactions to the disclosure, in June 2014, that Facebook had allowed academic researchers to manipulate the news feeds of 689,000 users for one week. The experiment, in which half of the users saw fewer positive posts than usual and the other half saw fewer negative ones than usual, was designed to determine whether the changes would cause people to write more positive or negative posts themselves. In fact, the researchers did find evidence of "emotional contagion" and published the results in a prestigious scientific journal. But their findings were eclipsed by the public outcry.

Shortly after the story broke, the lead researcher issued a statement saying that he and his colleagues were sorry for the anxiety their work had caused. But Facebook defended its actions for days, explaining that the boilerplate language in its 9,000-word user agreement constituted informed consent. Nearly a week elapsed before the company's chief operating officer offered a half-hearted apology for "poorly communicating" about the study. Three months later, the chief technology officer issued another statement, saying Facebook had been "unprepared for the reaction," conceding, "there are things we should have done differently," and articulating new research guidelines. Still, he avoided the words "sorry" and "apologize."

In this episode, Facebook erred in two ways: First, it violated users' trust. Second, it compounded the problem with an awkward, three-step, not-very-contrite apology.

Scenarios like this are all too common. At some point, every company makes a mistake that requires an apology—to an individual; a group of customers, employees, or business partners; or the public at large. And more often than not, organizations and their leaders fail to apologize effectively, if at all, which can severely damage their relationships with stakeholders and their reputations, especially if the incidents become public (and publicized).

Companies need clear guidelines for determining whether a misstep merits an apology and, when it does, how to deliver the message. In this article, we present an apology formula, drawn from our work and research in management and psychology, that provides a diagnostic and practical guidance on the who, what, where, when, and how of an effective apology. The bottom line for serious transgressions: Senior leaders must immediately express candor, remorse, and a commitment to change in a high-profile setting—and make it sincere.

The Apology Dilemma

Let's recognize two facts about apologies at the outset: First, we are psychologically predisposed to find reasons (or excuses) to delay or avoid saying we're sorry. Apologizing feels uncomfortable and risky. There's a loss of power or face involved—it rearranges the status hierarchy and makes us beholden, at least temporarily, to the other party. That doesn't feel good. So it's no wonder people try to avoid dwelling on or drawing attention to mistakes and that when one is pointed out, they get defensive, arguing their side of the story and shifting blame to others.

Apologies are even more difficult in an organizational context. When considering whether and how to apologize, even seasoned leaders can become gripped by indecision. That's understandable. A company mistake is often caused by a single division or employee,

Idea in Brief

The Problem

Organizations often struggle to get apologies right. Many leaders fear that an apology could expose their firm to legal action; others offer a cursory "I'm sorry" without addressing victims' concerns. Bungling an apology is costly, resulting in damaged reputations and relationships.

The Solution

Companies need clearer guidelines for determining whether a mistake merits an apology and, when it does, for crafting and delivering an effective message.

The Formula

Ask four questions: Was there a violation? Was it core to our promise or mission? How will the public react? Are we committed to change? Then think carefully about the who, what, where, when, and how of executing the apology.

and a bad situation is frequently made worse by events beyond its control. It can feel unjust for a CEO or an entire organization to have to take responsibility.

Second, companies have a strong tendency to evaluate the situation through a legal lens. Corporate counsel may fixate on whether any laws were broken and warn managers that an apology might be construed as an admission of liability (possibly exposing the company to litigation) rather than as an effort to empathize with the wronged party. This is an important distinction, because effective apologies address the recipients' feelings—they don't prove a point. Unfortunately, a litigious perspective has become ingrained in many organizations: Even a leader who isn't actively consulting with an attorney may worry that an apology could create legal problems.

Companies need to stop thinking this way. Most apologies are low cost—and many create substantial value. They can help defuse a tense situation, and fears of litigation are often unfounded. Consider health care providers. For many years, medical professionals were advised not to apologize when they made mistakes that hurt or even killed patients, because doing so might make the hospital vulnerable to a malpractice lawsuit. But research has revealed that when some hospitals began allowing doctors to offer apologies to patients and families, or even made apologizing mandatory, the likelihood of litigation was *reduced*.

Should You Apologize?

If a company is debating whether or not to apologize, managers should consider the nature and severity of the violation and the costs and benefits of offering an apology. Four questions can help determine if an apology is necessary.

1. Was there a violation, whether real or perceived?

When a company apologizes, it accepts full or partial blame for causing harm. So it needs to first determine whether a violation has in fact occurred and if so, whether the company is responsible. But here's the tricky part—this needs to be done quickly and perceptions of responsibility matter.

Consider the crisis Coca-Cola faced in 1999. It began on June 8, when a schoolboy in Belgium reported feeling ill after drinking a Coke. Within days, hundreds of people had attributed fevers, dizziness, and nausea to Coca-Cola beverages, and many made their way to hospitals. At first, the company insisted that its products did not pose a health risk and that bad carbon dioxide at a plant in Antwerp had triggered unnecessary alarm. CEO M. Douglas Ivester, hoping that the crisis would "blow over," said that he'd decided to "take a lower profile on this." But by the end of the week, the company was forced to remove more than 50 million beverages from the shelves in France, Germany, and Belgium. Finally, more than a week after the first incident, Ivester said publicly that he and his executives "deeply regret any problems encountered by our European consumers."

If we put ourselves in Ivester's shoes, we can easily understand why Coca-Cola might have had trouble making a quick decision about whether to apologize. First, we'd all prefer to see the results of an internal investigation and understand exactly what caused the bad outcome—and how to prevent it from happening again—before making any statements. Second, we'd be just as likely to hope that the issue would fade from attention. And third, we'd probably feel defensive and that we'd been unfairly blamed. The senior executives at Coca-Cola honestly believed that the reported health concerns were exaggerated and that many of the complaints had nothing to do with their products.

But companies must overcome the tendency to wait, to keep a low profile, or to argue the facts. Instead, leaders should consider others' perceptions of the potential violation and move swiftly to address them. An apology enables an executive to express concern and convey the organization's values—even as an investigation into exactly what happened and who was responsible unfolds.

As we make the apology decision, we need to consider the "psychological contract"—the expectations customers, employees, business partners, or other stakeholders have about an organization's responsibilities and what is right or fair. This often extends well beyond any explicit contract. To understand those expectations, managers have to imagine the situation from different vantage points.

Consider Mattel's launch of Hello Barbie, a doll that records and uploads conversations to Mattel online so that it can make personalized responses. Mattel thought that the doll's ability to remember a child's name and preferences would be a unique selling point, but critics quickly voiced privacy concerns. Mattel never intended to cause harm, but consumers' perceptions of an "eavesdropping Barbie" were so negative that it was forced to offer public reassurances to customers that Mattel was committed to safety and security. Presumably, leaders could have predicted that a toy that recorded children's play and uploaded it to the company would raise flags. In the Facebook situation, had the company considered the perspectives of its stakeholders before launching its emotion manipulation study, it might have avoided much of the fallout. And Coca-Cola should have known that even the perception of health concerns related to its products should be addressed immediately.

2. Was the violation core or noncore?

Certain activities and responsibilities are central to a company's products, services, and mission. Other responsibilities are peripheral or less consequential. If an automaker's vehicles contain a flaw that imperils drivers' safety or a restaurant's diners suffer food poisoning, those are core violations. When the accounting firm Arthur Andersen certified Enron's financial statements and failed to expose the company's massive fraud, it violated its core responsibility.

Other violations might involve a business function that's outside the company's operational core. For instance, Apple and other companies have been criticized for using transfer pricing and other financial tools to minimize their tax bills—a practice that offends people who see paying taxes as a civic duty. Although it constitutes a violation for at least some of their consumers, it is not core, because tax accounting is not those companies' central activity.

Core violations pose a fundamental threat to the mission of the organization. Therefore, a robust apology is critical—and a botched one can cause significant damage. A company that has committed a noncore violation has greater flexibility, though an apology may still be warranted or beneficial.

3. How will the public react?

Sometimes violations that harm only a single person or a small group can remain private matters. But remember, thanks to Twitter, Instagram, Yelp, Facebook, and other social media outlets, a single customer complaint can easily go viral and influence the perceptions of millions of potential customers. Even the smallest transgressions can blow up into epic (and costly) public relations nightmares.

Consider what happened to United Airlines in 2008. The company allegedly damaged a Canadian singer's guitar during a flight from Halifax to Nebraska and then subjected him to a Kafkaesque customer service experience. In the pre-internet era, the public would probably never have learned about the incident. Social media has changed that: In this case, the frustrated singer wrote a song called "United Breaks Guitars" and posted a video of it on YouTube. It became a sensation, with nearly 15,000 views its first day and more than 14 million since. Eventually, Rob Bradford, United's managing director of customer solutions, telephoned the singer and apologized directly; he also asked if the airline could use the video to help improve its customer service.

In gauging the probable reaction to an incident, companies should take into account the relative size and status of the parties. A violation committed by a large, powerful, or high-status organization (such as United, Google, Walmart, or the U.S. government) against a low-status, low-power person or group is more likely to engender public outrage—and require an apology—than a violation committed by a mom-and-pop business or one that hurts only wealthy individuals or corporations.

4. Is the company willing to commit to change?

In assessing whether or not to apologize, organizational leaders must also focus on the extent to which they are willing—and able—to change the company's behavior. If they can't or don't want to do things differently in the future, the case for making an apology is weak, because it will sound hollow and unconvincing.

When Target and Home Depot suffered cyber-security breaches that exposed customers' credit card information to hackers, the companies' apologies would have been ineffective without promises to institute procedures to prevent a reccurrence. (For a look at instances when it makes sense for companies to stand firm in the face of perceived harm, see the sidebar "The Power of Being Unapologetic.")

Sometimes managers become so focused on their new course of action that they forget to apologize. That's a mistake; without a show of remorse, people are likely to think you're whitewashing the violation.

The Apology Formula: The Right Way to Apologize

Once a company has decided that it should apologize, it has to do it right. It's astonishing how many well-intentioned, sophisticated organizations completely botch apologies. While a good apology can restore balance or even improve relationships, a bad apology can make things much worse. As a framework for getting it right, companies need to think carefully about who, what, where, when, and how.

Get Your Apology Right the First Time

Do Convey Remorse

"Today's GM will do the right thing. That begins with my sincere apologies to . . . the families and friends [of those] who lost their lives or were injured. I am deeply sorry."

—Mary Barra, CEO, GM, in 2014 testimony to the U.S. Congress in the wake of the company's ignition-switch recall

Don't Be Tone Deaf

"We're sorry for the massive disruption it's caused to [people's] lives. There's no one who wants this thing over more than I do. I want my life back."

—Tony Hayward, then CEP, BP, in 2010 after a rig explosion caused the biggest oil spill in U.S. history

Do Show Candor

"We've been doing a terrible job . . . meeting demand for our products. . . . We suck at this. I suck at this. I apologize to all of you. . . ."

—Min Liang-Tan, CEO, Razer, after missing the April 2014 shipping date for its gaming laptop

Don't Address the Wrong Victim

"I'm sad for the people of Lululemon who . . . had to face the brunt of my actions. I'm sorry to have put you all through this."

—Chip Wilson, Founder, Lululemon, in 2013, after blaming his company's see-through yoga pants fiasco on the women who wear them

Do Get the Message Out

"You count on us at JetBlue . . . and we know we let some of you down . . . and for that we are truly sorry."

—Rob Maruster, then-COO, JetBlue, in a 2011 YouTube apology to passengers who'd been stranded on the tarmac for nearly eight hours

---

Who

The more serious and the more core the violation, the more necessary it becomes that a senior leader—up to and including the CEO—make the apology. In cases where there is a clear transgressor—an employee who made the mistake—there may be merit in involving that person. But if he or she isn't sufficiently senior, you risk

The Power of Being Unapologetic

SOMETIMES AN UNAPOLOGETIC STANCE makes sense. Consider these examples:

- John Chambers, the former CEO of Cisco, was criticized for how he handled innovation at the company. He assembled teams to create small start-up companies that Cisco would later buy at predetermined prices—a practice that made some employees very wealthy and others extremely resentful. But Chambers wouldn't apologize, because he had a message to send: Innovation was more important to him than equitable pay.

- Although fast-food giant McDonald's has responded to concerns about the nutritional content of its food with more-healthful menus and smaller portion sizes, it took a new stance in a recent marketing campaign. Its ads unapologetically promote the Big Mac as "not Greek yogurt" and as a sandwich that "will never be kale."

When leaders and corporations embrace their values and identity—unapologetically—they stand to gain credibility and power.

---

offending the wronged party or the public by conveying that you are not taking the violation seriously. Just as it's better to be overdressed than underdressed, when in doubt, you should err on the side of having a senior executive offer the apology.

For example, Target released a statement from then-CEO Gregg Steinhafel the day after its security breach came to light. When a plane full of JetBlue passengers was stranded on a runway for eight hours, it was then-COO Rob Maruster who issued the apology on YouTube.

Deciding who should receive the apology is often straightforward—although companies can slip up here too. Consider the video that Chip Wilson, the founder of Lululemon, released during the furor over an interview in which he had said that his brand's yoga pants weren't suitable for some bodies. His "I'm sorry to have put you all through this" was addressed to employees, not customers, and was roundly criticized. Effective apologies are delivered directly to the person or people harmed. When that group is large and diffuse, the organization might want to offer an "open" apology through the press or social media.

What

This is the substance of the apology—the words you say and the actions you take. It's important to keep three goals in mind: candor, remorse, and a commitment to change.

The best apologies show *candor*. They leave no room for equivocation or misinterpretation, and they make absolutely clear that the organization acknowledges both the harm that was caused and its own responsibility. Consider the candid apology Razer's CEO gave after severe delays for preorders of the company's Blade laptop in 2014. "We've been doing a terrible job anticipating and meeting demand for our products . . . We suck at this. I suck at this. I apologize to all of you who have had to wait for ages each time we launch a new product."

Organizations should never sound defensive or as if they're trying to justify a violation. However, explanations and information can help. For instance, an airline's apology for a mechanical delay is more effective if the airline explains exactly what part is broken, what's being done to fix it, how much time it will take, and why the issue will pose no safety risk once fixed. Military condolence letters— a form of institutional apology—routinely offer details regarding the circumstances of the mission on which the soldier was killed. After receiving some information, those affected have a greater appreciation for the broader context and the institution's perspective.

Effective apologies also express *remorse*. We've criticized Facebook's handling of the emotion manipulation study, but in 2006, when users were upset by the company's just-launched News Feed feature, CEO Mark Zuckerberg offered a pitch-perfect apology. "We really messed this one up," his written statement began. He went on to use phrases like "bad job," "errors," "we missed this point," "big mistake," and "I'm sorry." He even thanked groups that had formed to protest. "Even though I wish I hadn't made so many of you angry, I am glad we got to hear you." His choice of words was remorseful and self-abasing—and effective.

The third key ingredient is demonstrating *a commitment to change*. An apology should create distance from the "old self" that committed the violation and establish a "new self" that will not engage in similar behavior. Sometimes the employee responsible for an error is fired. Sometimes, as in the Target and Home Depot security breaches, new procedures are put in place. Organizations might also demonstrate a seriousness of purpose by appointing an independent authority to investigate the incident and recommend changes—and pledging to implement the recommendations.

Consider how the Vancouver Taxi Association responded in 2014 after a cab driver left a mother and her sick child on the side of the road after he realized that they intended to pay for their ride from a local hospital to the airport with a hospital-issued taxi voucher, which he didn't believe his cab company would accept. (In fact it would.) Not only did the taxi association express remorse for the incident, it demonstrated a commitment to change by suspending the driver and instituting a clear policy instructing all cabs to accept all vouchers from local hospitals at all times.

Now let's consider an apology that lacked the three "what" elements: candor, remorse, and a commitment to change. In 2009, Goldman Sachs CEO Lloyd Blankfein issued a vague apology for unspecified acts by the financial industry that led to the Great Recession. His language was roundly criticized. As the *New York Times* editorialized, "His remarks do not come close to an apology . . . since he never actually said what he was sorry for . . . or to whom he was apologizing." Nor did he explain how the bank would change its behavior.

Blankfein learned his lesson, however. After this very public rebuke, he held another press conference, in which he admitted that Goldman had participated "in things that were clearly wrong and we have reasons to regret and apologize for." The firm pledged $500 million to help small businesses recover from the recession. This apology was far more candid, expressed remorse, and demonstrated a commitment to change.

Where

If a company wants to control the coverage of an apology, the setting can determine how loud—and widely heard—the message will be. Organizations often default to written statements that reach a broad audience, especially when they're published in newspapers. Target did this following its security breach, as did News International after some of its newspapers were found to have illegally hacked phones. For a more personal touch, the CEO or another executive might videotape an on-camera statement, as JetBlue's Maruster did. A live statement, with or without an audience, increases the perceived importance of the apology. In some instances, it may even make sense for leaders to travel to the place where the violation happened—a crash site, the location of an industrial accident, and so on. This not only provides a camera-ready backdrop, but also it shows that the executive cares enough to view the damage firsthand and apologize to victims in person. For example, when a Southwest Airlines flight overshot the runway at Chicago's Midway Airport in 2005, killing a six-year-old boy and injuring others, CEO Gary Kelly immediately flew to Chicago, visited the hospital, held a press conference, and offered several apologies, winning high marks for sensitivity.

Managers should realize, however, that there are risks to this approach. A live, on-site apology puts a leader in an uncontrolled environment. Apologizing to victims face-to-face can be effective if they accept the apology—but if they don't, the event could turn into a public confrontation. Sometimes public apologies come off as publicity stunts. Social media has changed the calculus for choosing where to make an apology, since now a company's written statement can be shared and retweeted, reaching many more people than would typically see an address on the evening news.

When

A good apology arrives quickly. Speed signals sincerity and dispels the idea that executives feel uncertainty or ambiguity about their responsibility. Sometimes, companies delay apologies for good reasons, such as Coke's desire, in 1999, to investigate customers' health concerns and their root cause. Facebook's intention to present a fully-formed plan to show its commitment to change appears to have been one factor in its slow apology for the emotion-manipulation study. The desire to be cautious is reasonable, but we believe that it's better to offer a quick "placeholder" apology than to be silent.

"While we're still gathering the facts to understand exactly what took place, we want our customers and employees to know that we apologize for any harm we have caused. Know that we are developing plans to ensure that this doesn't happen again. We will follow up by the end of the week with details."

While speedy apologies are preferable, the window of opportunity for apologizing never completely closes, and for many victims a belated apology is better than none at all. Consider the well-received statement made by GM's Mary Barra after the company's 2014 recall of faulty ignition switches—a problem the company had known about, but not acted on, for 10 years: "Today's GM will do the right thing . . . I am deeply sorry." Barra also told employees that the violation was "unacceptable"; 15 leaders deemed responsible for the cover-up were let go. If a previous CEO decided not to offer an apology for a violation but the new CEO believes one is warranted, the organization should make one regardless of the time lag.

How

The way an apology is delivered can matter just as much as the content of the apology. Informal language and personal communication can help. Recall Zuckerberg's use of the phrase "We really messed this one up."

Or consider what happened when DiGiorno pizza used the hashtag #WhyIStayed to promote its pizzas, not realizing that the tag was already being used by women to share their experiences of abuse. The company not only deleted its initial tweet but also followed it with another: "A million apologies. Did not read what the hashtag was about before posting." It sent direct tweets to every person who had expressed outrage: "@ejbrooks It was. And I couldn't be more sorry for it, Emma. Please accept my deepest apologies."

Written statements have the benefit of being broadcast quickly, but it is often easier to strike the right tone through speech. A leader can rely on nonverbal cues to convey emotion, humility, and empathy. For example, remorse can be shown through facial expressions, and a commitment to change reinforced through vigorous gestures.

But in-person apologies are tricky to master. It can be difficult for business leaders accustomed to displaying power and self-confidence to strike the right repentant tone. For some, it may require careful planning and rehearsal. One glaring example of a leader who got the "how" of his apology wrong is Tony Hayward, then-CEO of BP. During the catastrophic Deepwater Horizon oil spill, in the Gulf of Mexico, he delivered the following apology: "We're sorry for the massive disruption it's caused to [people's] lives. There's no one who wants this thing over more than I do. I'd like my life back." It was a strikingly tone-deaf remark, one that illustrates the danger of an off-the-cuff or improvised apology. (Hayward resigned a few weeks later.)

Preparing to Apologize

As a general rule, the more central to the mission of the company the violation is and the more people it affects, the more important it is that the apology be pitch-perfect. For core violations, the "what" has to show a tremendous commitment to change, the "who" has to be senior leaders, the "when" has to be fast, the "where" has to be high profile, and the "how" must be deeply sincere and demonstrate empathy.

There are some industries that apologize so frequently that they have the practice down to a science. Restaurants inevitably make mistakes—taking an order incorrectly, preparing the wrong dish, miscalculating the bill—and diners have come to expect a quick visit and an apology from the manager, along with a small offering (often a free dessert) as a consolation. When a Ritz-Carlton hotel failed to deliver a wake-up call at the appointed hour, causing a guest to run late for an important meeting, the front desk manager immediately apologized and offered to send up a complimentary breakfast. When the guest returned that evening, she found a handwritten apology from the general manager, fresh strawberries, dried fruit, and candy. Rather than lambaste the hotel, she raved to her friends about the five-star service she received.

It's imperative to give forethought to the kinds of events that will create the need for an organizational apology and how it will be executed. We recommend role-playing and "apology rehearsals." Making these investments is not strictly about damage control: A well-executed apology can improve relationships with customers, employees, and the public, leaving the company better positioned than it was before the error. That's an outcome to which every leader should aspire.

Originally published in September 2015. Reprint R1509B

About the Contributors

ALISON WOOD BROOKS is the O'Brien Associate Professor of Business Administration at Harvard Business School.

RYAN W. BUELL is a professor of business administration in the Technology and Operations Management unit at Harvard Business School, where he is the faculty chair of the Transforming Customer Experiences Executive Education program.

ANNE SIEBOLD DRAPEAU is the Chief People Officer at Toast, Inc. She is a coauthor, with Robert M. Galford, of *The Trusted Leader*.

FRANCES X. FREI is the UPS Foundation Professor of Service Management at Harvard Business School and a coauthor of *Unleashed: The Unapologetic Leader's Guide to Empowering Everyone Around You* (Harvard Business Review Press, 2020).

THEODORE "THEO" FORBATH is a managing director at Accenture.

ROBERT M. GALFORD is a managing partner at the Center for Leading Organizations is a leadership fellow. He is a coauthor of *Simple Sabotage: A Modern Field Manual for Detecting & Rooting Out Everyday Behaviors That Undermine Your Workplace*.

ADAM D. GALINSKY is the chair of the Management Division at the Columbia Business School. He coauthored the book *Friend & Foe* and delivered the TED talk "How to Speak Up for Yourself."

SHALENE GUPTA is a research associate at Harvard Business School. She is a coauthor of *The Power of Trust*.

LESLIE K. JOHN is a professor of business administration at Harvard Business School.

RODERICK M. KRAMER is a social psychologist and the William R. Kimball Professor of Organizational Behavior at the Stanford Graduate School of Business.

BETH A. LIVINGSTON is an associate professor of management and entrepreneurship at the University of Iowa's Tippie College of Business. She and Tina Opie are the authors of *Shared Sisterhood* (Harvard Business Review Press, 2022).

TIMOTHY MOREY is Global Managing Director at frog, a global product strategy and design firm.

ANNE MORRISS is an entrepreneur and the executive founder of the Leadership Consortium. She is a coauthor of *Unleashed: The Unapologetic Leader's Guide to Empowering Everyone Around You* (Harvard Business Review Press, 2020).

TINA OPIE is an expert in leadership and culture, diversity, equity, and inclusion; an associate professor of management at Babson College; and a visiting scholar at Harvard Business School. She is a coauthor, with Beth Livingston, of *Shared Sisterhood* (Harvard Business Review Press, 2022).

ALLISON SCHOOP is former Head of Strategy, San Francisco, at frog, a global product strategy and design firm.

MAURICE E. SCHWEITZER is the Cecilia Yen Koo Professor at the Wharton School and a coauthor of *Friend & Foe*. His research interests include negotiations, emotions, and deception.

SANDRA J. SUCHER is a professor of management practice at Harvard Business School. She is a coauthor of *The Power of Trust*.

PAUL J. ZAK is the founding director of the Center for Neuroeconomics Studies and a professor of economics, psychology, and management at Claremont Graduate University. He is also the CEO of Immersion Neuroscience and the author of *Trust Factor*.

JAMIL ZAKI is an associate professor of psychology at Stanford University, the director of the Stanford Social Neuroscience Laboratory, and the author of *The War for Kindness: Building Empathy in a Fractured World*. He studies human connections, what they do for us, and how people and organizations can learn to connect better.

Index

The most important management ideas all in one place.

We hope you enjoyed this book from *Harvard Business Review*. Now you can get even more with HBR's 10 Must Reads Boxed Set. From books on leadership and strategy to managing yourself and others, this 6-book collection delivers articles on the most essential business topics to help you succeed.

HBR's 10 Must Reads Series

The definitive collection of ideas and best practices on our most sought-after topics from the best minds in business.

- Change Management
- Collaboration
- Communication
- Emotional Intelligence
- Innovation
- Leadership
- Making Smart Decisions

- Managing Across Cultures
- Managing People
- Managing Yourself
- Strategic Marketing
- Strategy
- Teams
- The Essentials

hbr.org/mustreads

Buy for your team, clients, or event.
Visit hbr.org/bulksales for quantity discount rates.